THE ART OF GUM PASTE FLOWER MAKING

Published in 1989 by LESOME PRESS
3 Tannery Court
Richmond Hill
Ontario, Canada
L4C 7V5

Revised edition of *Gum Paste Flower Making*, first published in 1985.

© Copyright 1989

ISBN 0-969-2523-2-3

Design and Production: Falcom Design and Communications Inc.

Line Illustrations: Lily Con

Editing: Caroline Stephens

Typing and Typesetting: Patty Sandquist and Attic Typesetting

Printed and bound in Canada by Maracle Press Limited

TABLE OF CONTENTS

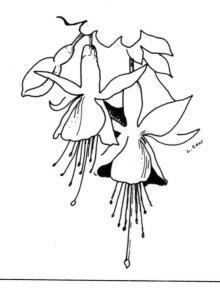

INTRODUCTION

Flowers. The world over, they express love, friendship and beauty. Can you imagine Valentine's Day without roses? A wedding without bouquets and adorned cake tops? Or *any* special occasion—a birthday, an anniversary, Christmas or Easter—without flowers?

My own love of flowers led me to the art of gum paste flower making and arranging. Many people believe you have to be an artist to do this type of work. But this is far from the truth. Anyone with patience and imagination can master it.

The flowers and leaves included in this book provide a good sampling of some common and not-so-common flowers popular in gum paste arrangements. I have grouped the flowers in three main sections according to their status in typical arrangements—main flowers, secondary flowers and filler flowers. There is also a separate section on leaves.

This revised edition of my first book, *Gum Paste Flower Making,* has been expanded to include several new flowers and leaves, new recipes for gum paste, new tools and materials, and advice on getting started and how best to display each type of flower in arrangements. It should be remembered that these are suggestions only. Let imagination be your best guide.

Whether you are just starting out or adding a few more flowers to an established *repertoire,* I hope this wonderful art brings you as much joy as it has brought me.

Good luck!

Geraldine

Geraldine

GETTING STARTED

Before starting any of the projects in this book, you will need to equip yourself with some basic supplies. First and foremost, for any flower you plan to make, find a fresh flower or excellent colour photograph to use as your model. Some tools and materials are required for every flower: flower cutter(s) (specific to each flower), wire cutter(s), wire (gauges specified), gum paste (in appropriate colours), gum glue, dusting colours (appropriate to flower), ball tool (size specified), rolling pin and board, spatula, cornstarch and white fat. These and any other tools and materials required are listed with each project.

Unless otherwise indicated, all the supplies listed here can be purchased from cake decorating suppliers or ordered directly from:

Creative Cutters
3 Tannery Court
Richmond Hill, Ontario
Canada   L4C 7V5
(416) 883-5638

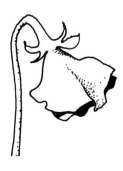

TOOLS AND MATERIALS

ALUMINUM FOIL
Used for shaping and drying flowers such as hibiscus and gardenias.

ANGER TOOL (Wooden)
Used for ruffling (e.g. carnations and orchid throats) and hollowing out the centres of some types of flowers (e.g. stephanotis and hyacinths).

BALL TOOL (Stylus, Metal)—Small
The ball tool or stylus has 2 different-sized balls, one at each end. One end of the mini-sized stylus is used for cupping miniature flowers such as forget-me-nots and lilies of the valley. The other end is used for cupping primroses and daisies.

BALL TOOL (Stylus, Metal)—Large
The larger-sized stylus is used, at one end, for roses and large-type petals, and at the other end, for sweet peas, small orchids and secondary flowers.

CARDBOARD TUBING
Used for semi-drying of petals and leaves.

CORN HUSK (Dried)
Make your own by drying a fresh corn husk and covering one side completely with masking tape to prevent the edges from curling. Used as a veining tool for orchid petals, leaves, calla lilies and any petals that require a straight vein.

CORNSTARCH (Any Brand) or Potato Starch
Available in supermarkets.
Used for ruffling and for gum paste creations. Sprinkle on the board to ease ruffling or lightly coat hands before hand-shaping of gum paste pieces.

CUTTERS

FLOWER CUTTERS
(Specific to each flower) Used for cutting the desired shape from gum paste.

CALYX CUTTER
Used for roses, sweet peas, carnations and any other flowers with a calyx.

WIRE CUTTERS (sharp, reliable)
Available from florist or garden shops as well as cake decorating suppliers. Essential for making clean cuts at the ends of the covered wires. Always cut the wires at an angle. This will help with the threading of the wires into the gum paste.

DOWEL (Round) 1/2″ to 3/4″ in diameter, 12″ long.
Available at lumber stores.
Used to obtain the desired petal shape (i.e. azaleas).
Note: Do not allow the petals to dry out on the dowel.

DUSTING COLOURS (Approved food colours only)
Used to give flowers a natural look. Highlight flowers by dusting them with Blossom Tints or Twinkle Dust.

FLORIST TAPE (Approximately 1/2″ wide)
Available in a variety of colours—pink, white, orange, lavender, brown and 4 shades of green—from hobby or florist supply shops.
Cut into 3 or 4 strips and use to cover various gauges of wire ensuring that the shiny side of the tape is next to the wire. Twist the wire and, at the same time, allow the tape to stretch as you attach it.

FLORIST WIRE
Available in 18″ lengths and in various gauges (thicknesses) from 16 to 32. (The lower the number, the thicker the wire.)
Available from hobby or florist supply shops.
Used as supports or stems for the blossoms or leaves.

FOAM (very soft, 2″ × 1/4″ thick)
Used to cushion small flowers such as forget-me-nots or any flowers that need cupping.

FOOD COLOUR
Used for colouring icing, fondant (sugar paste) and gum paste.

GELATIN POWDER or FINE CORN MEAL
Available in supermarkets.
Used to create the look of pollen on flowers such as the calla lily or open blown roses.

GUM GLUE
Use water, or better still, make your own gum glue using one part gum arabic to three parts water. Shake well and store in the refrigerator.
Used to join wet gum paste to wet gum paste or to join wet gum paste to dry gum paste. (Note: Use Royal icing only to join dry gum paste to dry gum paste.)

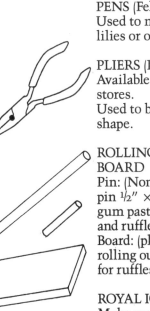

ICE CUBE TRAY, Small
Available at supermarkets or department stores.
Used for drying throats of moth orchids.

KNIFE (Artist's Palette Knife)
Available at art supply stores or from *Creative Cutters*.
Used for lifting the cut-out pieces of gum paste.

PAINT BRUSH (#3 watercolour brush)
Available at art supply stores or from *Creative Cutters*.
Used for painting gum glue onto petals.

PENS (Felt Tip, Food Colour)
Used to mark small dots on tiger lilies or orchid throats.

PLIERS (Long-Nosed)
Available at hardware or lumber stores.
Used to bend wire to the desired shape.

ROLLING PIN and NON-STICK BOARD
Pin: (Non-Stick, 8"-10" long or mini pin ½" × 4") Used for rolling out the gum paste or sugar paste for flowers and ruffles.
Board: (plastic preferred) Used for rolling out gum paste and sugar paste for ruffles.

ROYAL ICING
Make your own by mixing egg white with icing (powdered) sugar.

Used for dotting flowers such as tiger lilies and violets.

ROYAL ICING BAG (either nylon or parchment) with a #0 tip .

SPATULA
Used to lift gum paste petals or leaves off the board.

STAMENS
Available from hobby and florist supply shops.
Used for many flowers including freesias, open blown roses, azaleas and forget-me-nots.

STICK (Long, thin wooden shish-kebab stick)
Available in supermarkets.
Used for hollowing out small flowers such as hyacinths and stephanotis and also for curling back the edges of petals.

SUGAR, (Yellow)
Make your own from unflavoured gelatin and powdered food colour.
Used to create the colour in the stigma of calla lilies and for the yellow in irises.

THROAT HOLDER
Used for drying the throats of orchids for shaping.

TULLE
Available from dress supply or cake decorating shops.
Used to create the centres of daisies.

TWEEZERS (Bent-Nose)
Available at art supply stores or from *Creative Cutters*.
A must for arranging the flowers into bouquets. (They fit where fingers can't!)

VEINERS
Use leaves, plastic flower petals with good definition or make your own from modelling clay. First take an impression of a leaf in the clay, then allow the clay to dry or bake in the oven as directed on the package. Essential for giving leaves that natural look.

WHITE FAT (shortening, such as *Crisco*)
Available in supermarkets.
Used for light coating of gum paste board to ease rolling out of gum paste.

X-ACTO KNIFE
Used for ribbon insertion and for cutting out small designs in gum paste.

WHITE TAPE
Used instead of green florist tape for all white weddings.

RECIPES FOR GUM PASTE

Gum paste behaves differently in different climates, so do not be afraid to experiment by increasing or decreasing quantities of ingredients. Remember too that varying hand temperatures will have an effect on the behaviour of the paste.

The best way to achieve a natural look with gum paste flowers is to roll the paste very thinly and to use the right tools for the right job. The ball tool, for example, when used to thin the edges of the petals, disguises the cut edges.

SLOW DRYING GUM PASTE

An excellent paste for beginners. It dries slowly, thus extending the working time.

Mix together, completely dissolve, but DO NOT OVERHEAT

1 level Tbsp (15 ml) unflavoured gelatin
¼ cup (60 ml) cold water

Sift into a bowl

2 lbs (1,000 g) icing sugar (powdered sugar)
4 tsps (20 ml) gum tragacanth

Make a well in the centre of the bowl.

Method

Once the gelatin mixture has dissolved, add ½ cup (120 ml) of liquid glucose. Stir until free flowing and pour into the centre of the bowl. Working quite quickly, and with a spoon, stir the mixture and, at the same time, draw the sugar into the liquid. When about ½ the sugar has been incorporated, turn the mixture onto the counter and knead into it the remainder of the sugar. Place white fat on your hands

and knead the paste until it acquires an elastic consistency. Double wrap in plastic wrap, place in a plastic bag and store in the refrigerator. This recipe improves with age.

Note: You may require all the sugar. Test for readiness by holding gum paste in one hand. If it starts to fall down, add more sugar. If mixture is firm but soft, consistency is right.

FAST DRYING GUM PASTE

Perfect for experts. It dries almost the instant it is made. Flowers can be made same day.

Ingredients

¼ cup (60 ml) cold water
½ Tbsp (7.5 ml) gelatin
½ Tbsp (7.5 ml) liquid glucose
¾ lb (335 g) sifted icing sugar (Plus up to another ¾ lb (335 g) when gum paste is placed on table for kneading.)
1 Tbsp (15 ml) gum tragacanth

Method

Stand the gelatin in cold water for 2 minutes.
Sift the icing sugar and gum tragacanth together in a bowl.
Melt the gelatin over hot water. DO NOT OVERHEAT. Stir in the glucose.

Pour the warm liquid into the sugar, while continuing to stir the mixture. Turn out onto the table and knead. Place white fat onto hands and knead a few minutes. Wrap in plastic and store in the refrigerator.

PARTS OF THE FLOWER

BUD:
An undeveloped shoot
CALYX:
Outer Whorl of floral parts (sepals), usually green
COROLLA:
Inner circle of petals, usually coloured
PETAL:
A unit of the corolla, usually coloured
PISTIL:
Central organ (female of the flower including ovary, style and stigma)

SEPAL:
Segment of a calyx, normally green
STAMEN:
Pollen-bearing male organ
STAGES OF DEVELOPMENT:
buds
partly open
open blown

MAIN FLOWERS

ANEMONE
ANEMONE CORONARIA

Originally from the Eastern Mediterranean and Greece, these beautiful members of the buttercup family are also known as Wind Poppies or Lilies of the Field. Blooms come in white, mauve, purple and scarlet, with a central boss of stamens. Mixed strains include single "St. Brigid" and semi-double "de Caen" hybrids. Excellent as a main flower in arrangements for garden weddings, they can be blended with Pansies, Roses and/or Sweet Peas and accented with Green Ivy.

Parts of the Flower

multi-petalled, central boss of stamens, calyx

Tools and Materials

wire cutter
dogrose cutter
calyx cutter
24-gauge wire
gum paste
gum glue
dusting colours
ball tool
spatula
rolling pin and board
cornstarch
white fat
#1 paint brush
alcohol
apple tray for drying
black stamens
white white for painting

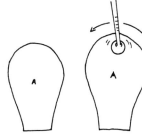

figure 1

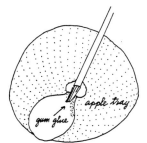

figure 3

figure 2

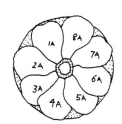

figure 4

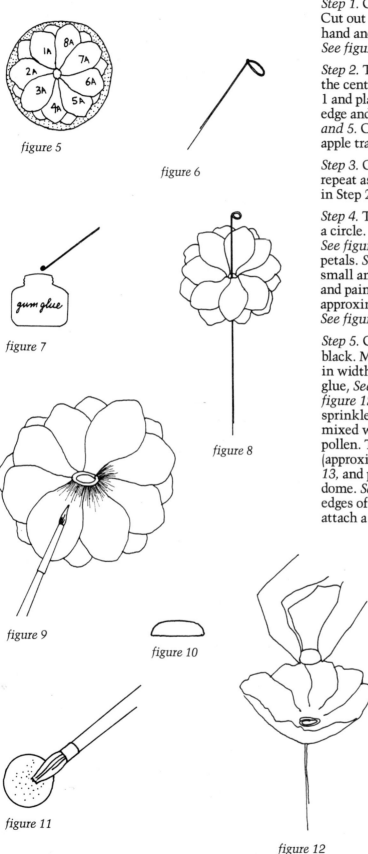

figure 5

figure 6

figure 7

figure 8

figure 9

figure 10

figure 11

figure 12

figure 13

figure 14

Method

Step 1. Colour the gum paste and roll out very thinly. Cut out 8 petals. Place one petal in the palm of your hand and, with the ball tool, thin around its top half. *See figure 1.*

Step 2. Take the apple tray and make a large hole in the centre. *See figure 2.* Take the first petal from Step 1 and place in the apple tray. Gum glue the lower edge and place the next petal on top. *See figures 3, 4 and 5.* Continue until all petals are used or until apple tray is full.

Step 3. Cut out another 8 petals the same size and repeat as in Step 1. Again, place petals as described in Step 2.

Step 4. Take the 24-gauge wire and form the top into a circle. *See figure 6.* Dip the circle into gum glue. *See figure 7.* Push the wire through the centre of the petals. *See figure 8.* With a #1 paint brush, mix a small amount of alcohol and white white together and paint very fine lines from the centre up to approximately ¼ to ⅓ of the the way up the petal. *See figure 9.*

Step 5. Colour a very small amount of gum paste black. Make a small dome approximately ½" (10 cm) in width. *See figure 10.* Paint the flat side with gum glue, *See figure 11,* and place on top of the wire. *See figure 12.* Paint the top white, gum glue then sprinkle the dome with black sugartex (or ungelatin mixed with black food powder) to give the illusion of pollen. Take the very small black-headed stamens (approximately 36—¼" (5 mm) in length) *See figure 13,* and place at random around the outer edge of the dome. *See figure 14.* Let dry. When dry, highlight the edges of the flower with dusting food colours and attach a green calyx.

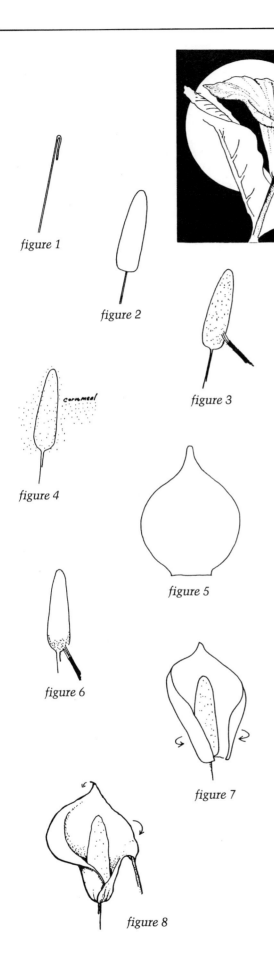

figure 1

figure 2

figure 3

figure 4

cornmeal

figure 5

figure 6

figure 7

figure 8

CALLA LILY
ZANTEDESCHIA AETHIOPICA

Known also as the Arum Lily or Lily of the Nile, this dramatically beautiful flower originated in South Africa. The flowers, 3-8 inches long on stout, leafless stems can be pure white, pink, red, yellow, peach or green. In arrangements, use alone embellished only with a Calla Lily leaf.

Parts of the Flower

spadix and spathe

Tools and Materials

calla lily cutter
wire cutter
24-gauge wire
gum paste
gum glue
dusting colours
ball tool
spatula
rolling pin and board
cornstarch
white fat
yellow-coloured gelatin powder or corn meal
small wooden stick

Method

Step 1. Form hook on the wire. *See figure 1.* Make a long sausage, slightly tapering one end. *See figure 2.* Paint with gum glue. *See figure 3.* Roll the sausage into the coloured gelatin or corn meal. *See figure 4.* Let dry.

Step 2. Roll out gum paste and cut out the flower. (Do not roll out very thinly as this flower has a waxy look.) Vein, then ball tool the edges. *See figure 5.*

Step 3. Dust the inside base of the petal with a soft yellow food colour. Paint the base of the sausage with gum glue. *See figure 6.* Wrap petal around the base of the sausage. *See figure 7.*

Step 4. Wrap the left side of the petal over the sausage and fold the right side over the left side. Take the wooden stick and curl the sides over the stick.

Step 5. Shape and bend the point of the flower slightly back. *See figure 8.* Let dry.

Step 6. The base and tip of the finished flower can be lightly dusted in a soft green. To give a final touch to the finished flower, steam over a boiling kettle to achieve a natural-looking waxy shine.

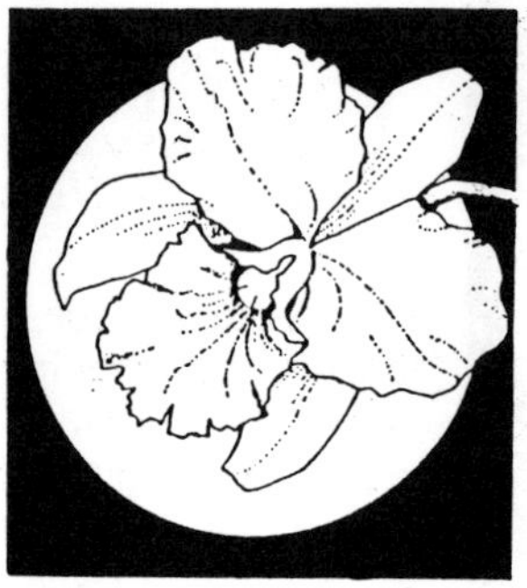

CATTLEYA ORCHID
CATTLEYA LABIATA

Native to South and Central America, this gorgeous flower, known as the "Queen" of orchids, was introduced into Britain from Brazil in 1818. There are 60 wild Cattleya species native to Central and South America. Cattleya orchids grow in a wide range of colours including various shades of red, yellow, purple, orange, white and their multi-coloured variations.

Parts of the Flower

column, throat, 2 petals, 3 sepals

Tools and Materials

cattleya cutters
wire cutters
veiner
throat holder
24-gauge wire
24-gauge wire (covered in white tape for white orchids)
gum paste
gum glue
dusting colours
ball tool
spatula
rolling pin and board
cornstarch
white fat
scissors
X-acto knife
wooden anger tool

Method

Step 1. To Make Column:
Note: The column of an orchid should never be longer than the distance from the bottom tip of the throat cutter to the first scallop.
Attach a long cylinder to the end of the hooked wire. *See figure 1.* Slightly taper the end of the column. *See figure 2.* Flatten the column a little and curl around the bottom end of the wooden anger tool. *See figure 3.* Take the X-acto knife and make a very slight cut mark approximately ¼" on either side of the column. *See figure 4.* Let dry.

figure 1

figure 2

figure 3

figure 4

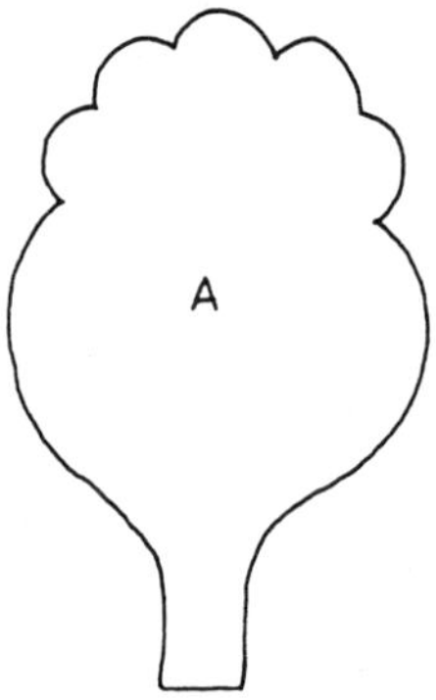

figure 5

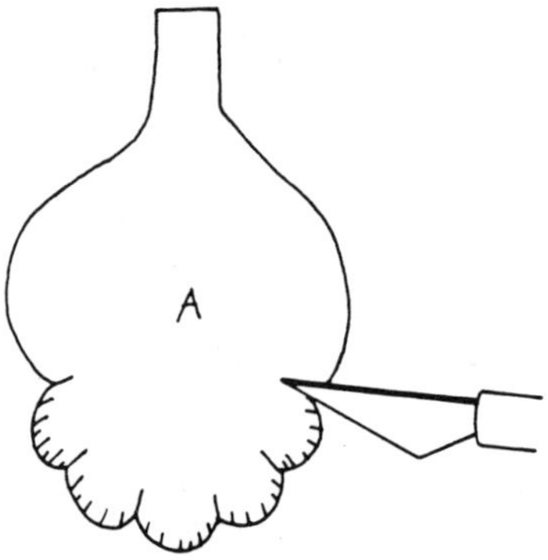

figure 6

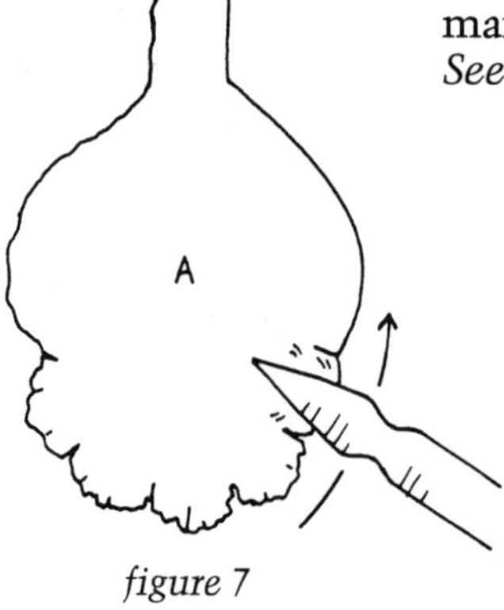

figure 7

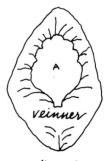

figure 8

Step 2. To Make Throat:
Roll out gum paste and cut out the throat of the orchid. *See figure 5.* With the X-acto knife, make little cuts in the scalloped part of the throat. *See figure 6.*

Step 3. Using the wooden anger tool, ruffle around the sides of the throat. *See figure 7.* Vein the throat. *See figure 8.*

Step 4. To Attach Column to Throat:
Paint the base and the sides of the column with gum glue. *See figure 9.* Attach the throat, making the join at the top of the column. *See figure 10.*

Step 5. Place the throat and column on the throat holder to dry. *See figure 11.*

Step 6. To Make Side Petals:
Roll out gum paste leaving a slightly thicker portion in the centre for threading the wire. Cut 2 side petals 'B.' *See figure 12.* With the anger tool, ruffle around the edges of each petal. *See figure 13.* Vein the petals.

Step 7. Holding the petals, thread the covered wire through the centre of the petals for approximately 1" of the petal, being careful not to let the wire break through. *See figure 14.* Shape petals to suit. (Either shape the petals so they curl inwards as in a semi-open flower or slightly backwards as in an open-blown flower.) Let dry.

Step 8. To Make Sepals:
Roll out gum paste and cut out 3 thin sepals. *See figure 15.* Thin around the edges using the ball tool. *See figure 16.* Vein, and very carefully thread the wire through the centre of the sepals. Shape the sepals to suit. Let dry.

Step 9. To Assemble Flower:
Chalk the throat of the flower and tape the 2 side (ruffled) petals 'B' to the throat. *See figure 17.* Position the 3 long sepals and tape to the throat and 'B' petals. *See figure 18.*

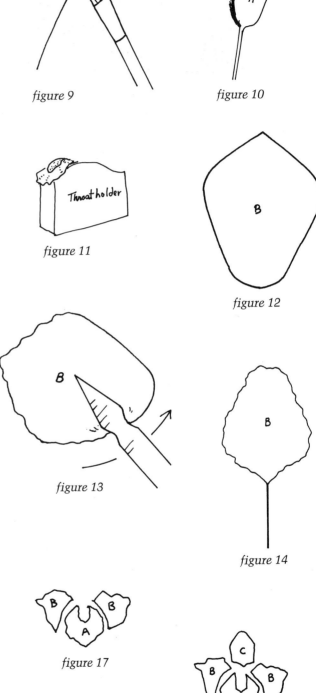

figure 9

figure 10

figure 11

figure 12

figure 13

figure 14

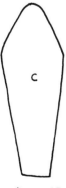

figure 15

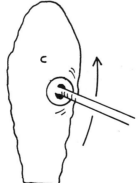

figure 16

figure 17

figure 18

CARNATION
DIANTHUS CARYOPHYLLUS

Originally from the Mediterranean region, these fragrant blooms with curled petal margins come in a wide range of colours—solid whites, yellows, pinks and reds, with mottled or striped variations. Carnations can be used as main flowers in arrangements or as secondary flowers with Roses or Sweet Peas. Green Ivy is an excellent compliment.

Parts of the Flower

multi-petalled with calyx

Tools and Materials

carnation cutter
calyx cutter
wire cutter
24 or 26-gauge wire (depending on the size of the carnation) A feathered carnation can be made on a 26-gauge wire.
gum paste
gum glue
dusting colours
ball tool
spatula
rolling pin and board
cornstarch
white fat
X-acto knife
wooden anger tool or round toothpick

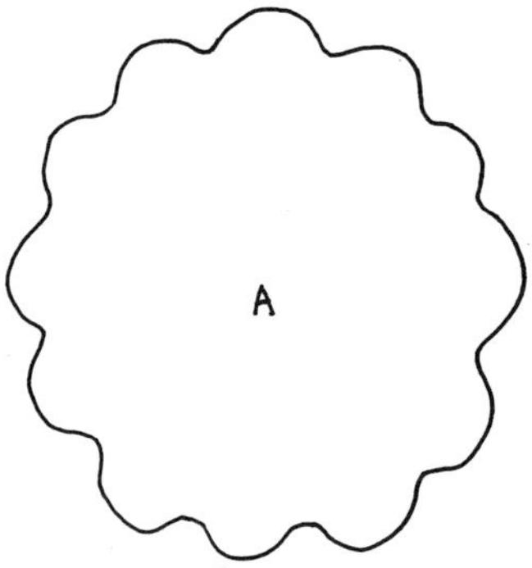

figure 1

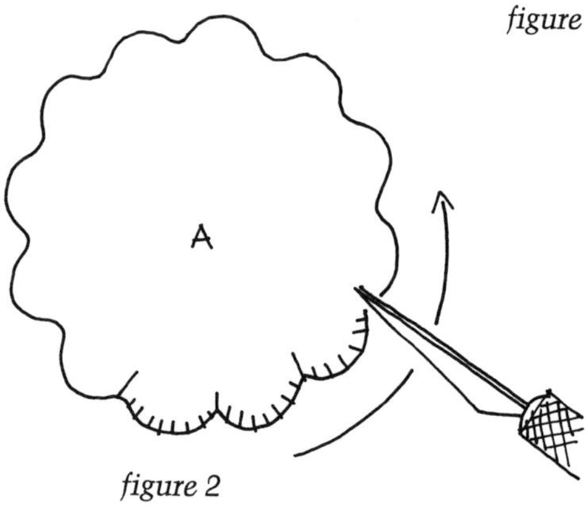

figure 2

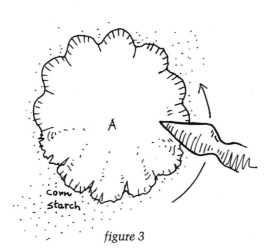

figure 3

figure 4

Method

Step 1. Cut out flower 'A.' *See figure 1.* With an X-acto knife, cut the edges of the petal with small cuts making a larger cut in the curve of the scallop. *See figure 2.*

Step 2. Place the flower on a small amount of corn starch and, with the wooden anger tool or a round toothpick, ruffle around the cut edges of the flower. *See figure 3.*

Step 3. Gum glue the centre of the flower. *See figure 4.* Fold the flower in half. *See figure 5.* Pleat the flower together and shape. *See figures 6 and 7.*

Step 4. Make a hook at the end of the wire and dip into gum glue. *See figure 8.* Pull the wire through the centre of the flower. *See figure 9.* Let dry.

Step 5. Roll paste very thin and cut out calyx. *See figure 10.* Gum glue calyx and wrap around the base of the flower. *See figure 11.*

figure 5

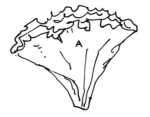

figure 6

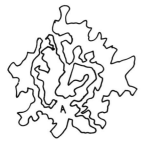

figure 7

figure 8

figure 9

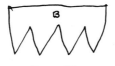

figure 10

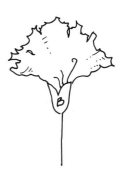

figure 11

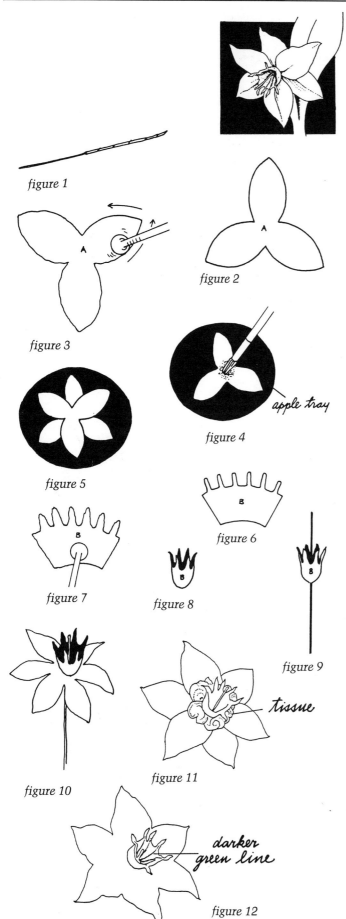

EUCHARIST LILY
EUCHARIS GRANDIFLORA

A magnificent, beautifully scented white flower, also known as the Amazon Lily, from the Andes of Colombia and Peru. Named for the Greek word meaning "very pleasing and filled with grace," these flowers look like snow-white Daffodils with lime green markings. Use alone as a main flower in arrangements, accented with Variegated Ivy.

Parts of the Flower

6 petals with a tendrilled trumpet

Tools and Materials

eucharist lily cutters
wire cutter
26-gauge wire
gum paste
gum glue
dusting colours
ball tool
spatula
rolling pin and board
cornstarch
white fat
yellow and green dusting colours
white stamens with no heads
apple tray

Method

Step 1. Tape a single stamen onto the 26-gauge wire. Set aside. *See figure 1.*

Step 2. Roll out the gum paste very thinly and cut out 2 sets of petals. Vein the petals and thin around the edges with the ball tool. *See figures 2 and 3.* Place the back 3 petals in the apple tray. Gum glue the centre, *See figure 4,* and place the front 3 petals on top. *See figure 5.* Make a hole in the centre.

Step 3. Roll out the gum paste very thinly and cut out the trumpet of the flower. *See figure 6.* With the ball tool, thin around the edges. *See figure 7.* Seam the sides together to form a cup. *See figure 8.* Shape onto the wire, cupping in the base. *See figure 9.* Gum glue the base and attach to the petals. *See figure 10.* Prop up the throat with tissue and let dry. *See figure 11.*

Step 4. Shade the inside of the trumpet with light lemon-green colour. Accent the tendrilled areas with a darker green. *See figure 12.*

FUCHSIA
FUCHSIA MACROSTEMMA

These dainty pendant flowers, native to Haiti, Santo Domingo, Mexico, southern Chile and Argentina, come in a fascinating variety of forms and a wonderful range of colours and colour combinations, from brilliant reds and purples to delicate, misty pastels. The flowers, borne either singly or in small terminal clusters, are single, semidouble or double. Because the Fuchsia is a very showy, vividly-coloured flower, it is best displayed by itself with Ivy or with small Roses.

Parts of the Flower

4 back sepals, front petals and stamens

Tools and Materials

fuchsia cutter
wire cutter
26-gauge wire
ball tool
gum paste
gum glue
dusting colours
ball tool
spatula
rolling pin and board
cornstarch
white fat
very small-headed stamens

figure 1

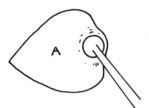

figure 2

figure 3

figure 4

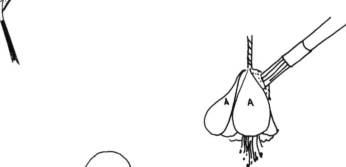

figure 9

figure 5

figure 6

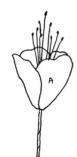

figure 7

figure 8

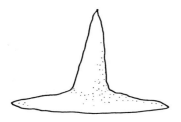

figure 10

figure 11

figure 12

figure 13

figure 14

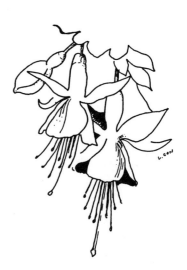

figure 15

figure 16

figure 17

Method

Step 1. Take 9 small stamens. Place them together in uneven lengths, making one extra long. Tape them on the wire. *See figure 1.* Place a small bud of gum paste over the join on which to stick the petals. Let dry. (This surface will be an easier one to which wet petals can be attached.)

Step 2. Roll out paste, very thinly, and cut out 4 'A' petals. *See figure 2.* Thin the edges of the petals using the ball tool, curling the edges slightly. *See figure 3.*

Step 3. Gum glue down one side of the petal. *See figure 4.* Continue overlapping approximately ⅓ of the petal. *See figure 5.* Join the petals together as illustrated. *See figure 6.* Wrap the petals around the wire. *See figure 7.* Let dry.
(Note: To make a double fuchsia, cut out 4 or 5 additional petals. Thin around the edges, then pinch the backs of the petals. *See figure 8.* Gum glue to the existing petals.) *See figure 9.*

Step 4. Cut out petal 'B' using the "Mexican Hat" method. *See figure 10.* Thin around the edges of petal 'B' with a ball tool. *See figure 11.*

Step 5. Slightly hollow the centre of petal 'B' with a ball tool. *See figure 12.* Gum glue the hollow centre of petal 'B.' *See figure 13.* Push the wire with petals 'A' attached through the centre of petal 'B.' *See figure 14.* Shape petals 'B' back away from petals 'A.'

Step 6. Shape a green hip. *See figure 15.* Gum glue the flat surface of the hip and pull through the wire. *See figures 16 and 17.*

GARDENIA
GARDENIA JASMINOIDES

Native to China and introduced in 1763, these gorgeous, powerfully scented flowers, also known as Cape Jasmine, were named after Dr. Alexander Garden, Scots correspondent of Linnaeus (1730-1791). The spirally-arranged double or single-formed blooms are waxy white. Excellent as a main flower in arrangements, Gardenias look lovely when complimented with Rose leaves or Green Ivy.

Parts of the Flower

multi-petalled

Tools and Materials

dogrose cutters
wire cutters
24-gauge green wire
28-gauge green wire
gum glue
gum paste
dusting colours
ball tool
spatula
rolling pin and board
cornstarch
white fat
apple tray

Method

Step 1. Colour a very small amount of gum paste a soft yellow. Cut the 28-gauge wire into 3 lengths, each approximately 4" (10 cm). Cover about ¼" (5 mm) of the tip of wire with the yellow paste to form a stamen. *See figure 1.* Shape into a slight crescent. Let dry. When dry, tape the 3 stamens to the 24-gauge wire. *See figure 2.*

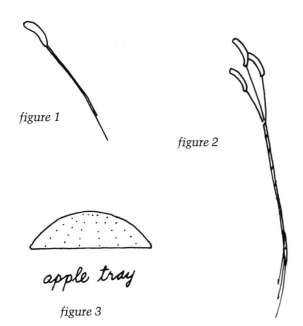

figure 1

figure 2

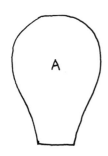

apple tray

figure 3

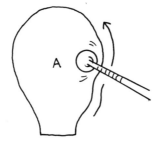

figure 4

A

figure 5

A

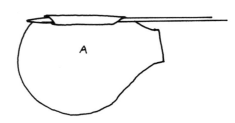

A

figure 6

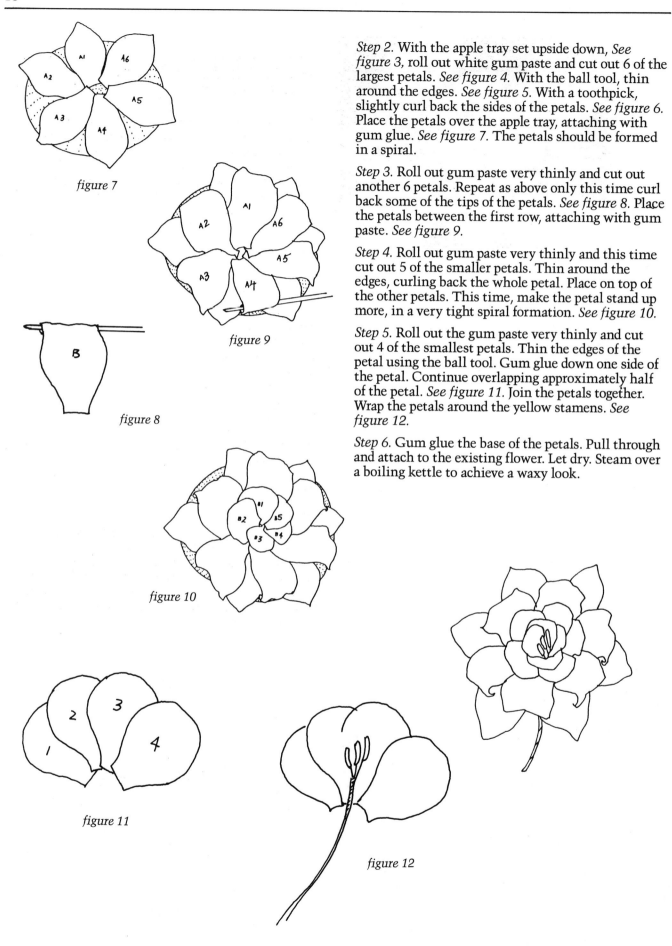

figure 7

figure 9

figure 8

figure 10

figure 11

figure 12

Step 2. With the apple tray set upside down, *See figure 3*, roll out white gum paste and cut out 6 of the largest petals. *See figure 4.* With the ball tool, thin around the edges. *See figure 5.* With a toothpick, slightly curl back the sides of the petals. *See figure 6.* Place the petals over the apple tray, attaching with gum glue. *See figure 7.* The petals should be formed in a spiral.

Step 3. Roll out gum paste very thinly and cut out another 6 petals. Repeat as above only this time curl back some of the tips of the petals. *See figure 8.* Place the petals between the first row, attaching with gum paste. *See figure 9.*

Step 4. Roll out gum paste very thinly and this time cut out 5 of the smaller petals. Thin around the edges, curling back the whole petal. Place on top of the other petals. This time, make the petal stand up more, in a very tight spiral formation. *See figure 10.*

Step 5. Roll out the gum paste very thinly and cut out 4 of the smallest petals. Thin the edges of the petal using the ball tool. Gum glue down one side of the petal. Continue overlapping approximately half of the petal. *See figure 11.* Join the petals together. Wrap the petals around the yellow stamens. *See figure 12.*

Step 6. Gum glue the base of the petals. Pull through and attach to the existing flower. Let dry. Steam over a boiling kettle to achieve a waxy look.

LARGE CYMBIDIUM ORCHID

Cymbidium, known as the "King" of Orchids, is one of the most popular Orchids today. It is found wild over a wide area from the foothills of the Himalayas to the coast of China and as far south as Australia, and has been cultivated since 1800. The name comes from the Greek *kymbe* (boat) and refers to the boat-like appearance of the lip. Cymbidium come in a wide range of colours from white, yellow and green to bronze, pastel and deep pinks. In arrangements, Cymbidium can be used either alone with small filler flowers or Roses accented with Variegated Ivy.

Parts of the Flower

column, throat, petals, 3 sepals

Tools and Materials

orchid cutters
orchid throat holder
wire cutter
24-gauge wire
gum paste
gum glue
dusting colours
ball tool
spatula
rolling pin and board
cornstarch
white fat
X-acto knife
scissors
apple tray

figure 1

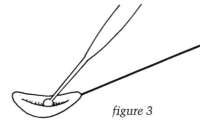

figure 2

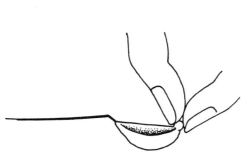

figure 3

figure 5

figure 4

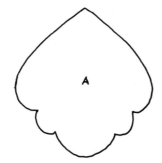

figure 6

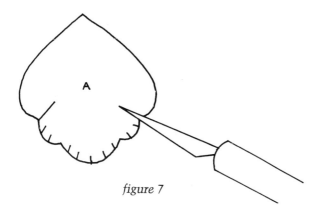

figure 7

Method

Step 1. To Make Column:
Note: The column of an orchid should never be longer than the distance from the bottom tip of the throat cutter to the first scallop.
Roll a small piece of gum paste into a flat-sided domed sausage approximately 1" in length. *See figure 1.* Dip the end of the wire into gum glue, *See figure 2,* and place onto the 24-gauge wire, pinching the end to secure to the wire. Hollow the flat side with a ball tool and bend the wire. *See figure 3.* Let dry. Roll out a tiny piece of paste ¼" in diameter. Gum glue the tip of the column and attach the small piece of paste, *See figure 4,* cutting through the centre to form 2 lips. *See figure 5.* Paint and colour the column until desired colour is achieved. Paint the surface of the hollow with dots. Let dry.

Step 2. To Make Throat:
Roll out the gum paste thinly and cut out the throat. *See figure 6.* Make small cuts around the scalloped part of the throat. *See figure 7.* Cut into the centre. Place the throat onto a lightly cornstarched board and ruffle the scalloped cut edge. *See figure 8.* Thin the plain edges with the ball tool and cup inwards. Place the trumpet onto an orchid throat holder. *See figure 9.* Allow to semi-dry. Gum glue the base of the column and place inside the trumpet. Let dry completely. *See figure 10.*

figure 10

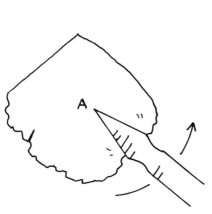

figure 8

apple tray

figure 11

throat holder

figure 9

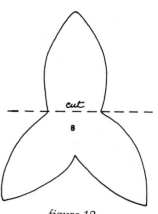

figure 12

Step 3. To Make Sepals:
Roll out gum paste and cut out the 3 back sepals.
Vein, thin around the edges with a ball tool, pinching
the top petal at the end. Then cup all 3 petals inwards.
Place inside an apple tray, *See figure 11.*

Step 4. To Make Lower Petals:
Roll out gum paste very thinly, and cut out the lower
2 petals. *See figure 12.* Vein, then thin around the
edges with a ball tool. Cup, from the back, the side
petals so that they fold 'backwards.' Gum glue and
place on top of the other back petals. *See figure 13.*
Make a hole through the centre of the petals. Gum
glue the base of the trumpet and place through the
hole. Lift the trumpet slightly with tissue paper until
completely dry. *See figure 14.*

Step 5. To Assemble Flower
When dry, paint and colour the trumpet, side and
back petals. Roll a piece of yellow gum paste into a
sausage approximately ¼" (5 mm) in diameter by ¾"
to 1" (15-20 mm) in length. Paint one end and place a
thin piece of wire down the length to form 2 lips. *See
figure 15.* Gum glue the sausage. Dip into a yellow
sugartex or yellow coloured gelatin and attach the
throat of the trumpet. *See figure 16.* Let dry.

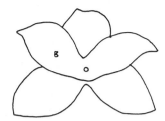

figure 13

figure 14

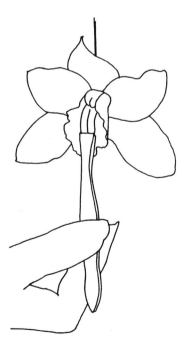

figure 16

yellow gumpaste

figure 15

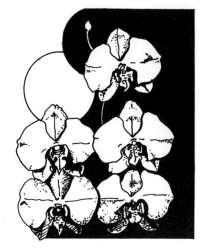

MOTH ORCHID
PHALANENOPSIS

Native to the Philippines, Burma, Eastern India, Borneo and New Guinea, these showy flowers come in a wide range of colours, both solid and multi-coloured, including white, pink, yellow, violet, mauve, red and orange. Moth Orchids look beautiful as main flowers in arrangements when complimented with Roses and Variegated Ivy.

Parts of the Flower

column, throat, 2 petals, sepals

Tools and Materials

moth orchid cutters
wire cutter
24-gauge wire
gum paste
gum glue
dusting colours
ball tool
spatula
rolling pin and board
cornstarch
white fat
small ice cube tray
scissors
wooden stick
styrofoam (preferred) or cardboard apple tray
Royal icing

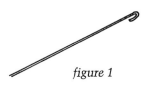

figure 1

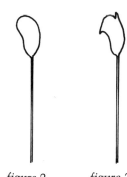

figure 2   *figure 3*

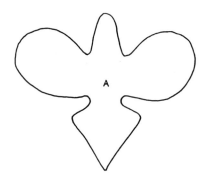

figure 4

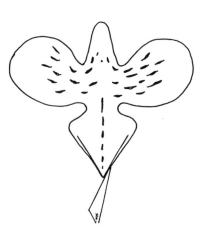

figure 6

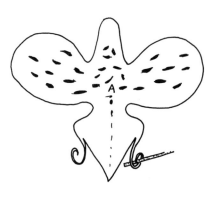

figure 7

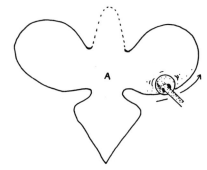

figure 5

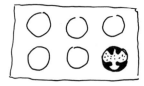

figure 8

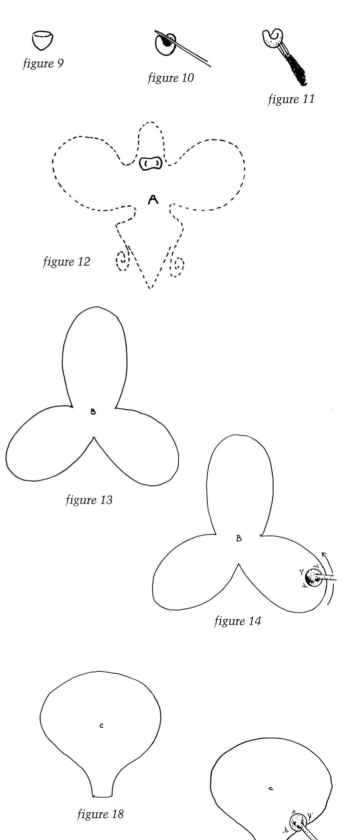

Method

Step 1. To Make Column:

Note: The column of an orchid should never be longer than the distance from the bottom tip of the throat cutter to the first scallop.

Make a very small hook at the end of the wire. *See figure 1.* Take a tiny piece of gum paste and place it over the hook. Slightly taper the paste to the wire, hollowing it out slightly at the top end. At the same time, pull the excess paste forward. *See figure 2.* Approximately ⅓ of the distance from the top of the point, cut a small 'V' with the scissors and lift open the point of the 'V.' *See figures 3.* Let dry.

Step 2. To Make Throat:

Roll out the gum paste very thinly and cut out the throat. *See figure 4.* Roll around the edges with the ball tool to thin the petals. However, do not thin the top of the petal (dotted area shown in *figure 5.*) Mark the throat with a non-toxic felt tip pen. With scissors, cut 2 very fine lines for tendrils. *See figure 6.* Take the wooden stick and curl the tendrils around the stick taking care not to break off the tendrils. *See figure 7.* Place the throat in an ice cube tray, cup the sides inwards and pack with tissue until dry. *See figure 8.*

Step 3. To Make 'Lips':

Take a very small piece of gum paste. *See figure 9.* Gently roll a wooden stick or toothpick back and forth in the centre to form the shape of a pair of lips. *See figure 10.* Paint the base of the lips with gum glue. *See figure 11.* Attach to the top of the throat in the centre of the 2 cupped side petals. *See figure 12.* Let dry.

figure 9

figure 10

figure 11

figure 12

figure 13

figure 14

figure 15

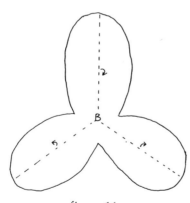

figure 16

figure 17

figure 18

figure 19

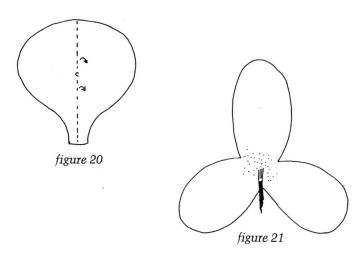

figure 20

figure 21

Step 4. To Make Back Petals:
Roll out gum paste very thinly and cut out the back petals. *See figure 13.* Thin around the edges with a ball tool. *See figure 14.* Vein. *See figure 15.* Gently fold the petals backwards and in half to create a creased effect. *See figure 16.* Place the petals in an apple tray. *See figure 17.* Set aside.

Step 5. To Make Side Petals:
Roll out gum paste very thinly and cut out the 2 side petals. *See figure 18.* Thin around the edges with a ball tool. *See figure 19.* Fold the petals in half and away from you, to create a creased effect. *See figure 20.*

Step 6. To Assemble Flower:
Paint the centre of the back petals with gum glue. *See figure 21.* Attach the 2 side petals as shown in *figure 22.* (As this flower is very flat looking, do not overshape the petals.) Paint the centre again with gum glue. *See figure 23.* Thread the throat through the centre of the petals. *See figure 24.* For side view, *see figure 25.* Let dry.

Step 7. Paint the thicker part of the top of the throat with gum glue. Attach the column. *See figure 26.* (If dry, use a small amount of Royal icing instead of gum glue.)

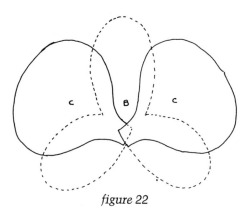

figure 22

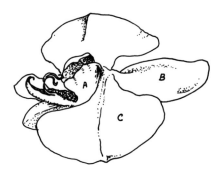

figure 25

figure 23

figure 24

figure 26

OPEN-BLOWN ROSE

Created with a combination of three different sizes of petals, these stunningly beautiful flowers are perfect in bridal arrangements complimented with Stephanotis or Sweet Peas and accented with Rose leaves.

Parts of the Flower

multi-petalled, calyx, hip

Tools and Materials

rose cutters
wire cutters
22- or 24-gauge wire
gum paste
gum glue
dusting colours
ball tool
spatula
rolling pin and board
cornstarch
white fat
knife
cardboard or styrofoam apple tray
very small yellow-headed stamens
spoons
7 tablespoons (Illustrated as 'A')
6 dessert spoons (Illustrated as 'B')
5 teaspoons (Illustrated as 'C')
or
varying sizes of glass marbles (instead of spoons)

Method

Step 1. Roll out gum paste very thinly. Cut out 7 large petals. Thin these around the edges with a large ball tool until the edges curl. Place each petal over the back of a tablespoon or glass marble to dry. (These are the 'A' petals.) *See figures 1, 2 and 3.*

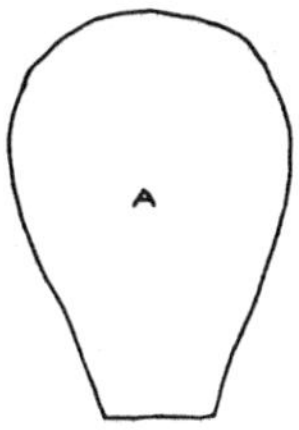

figure 1

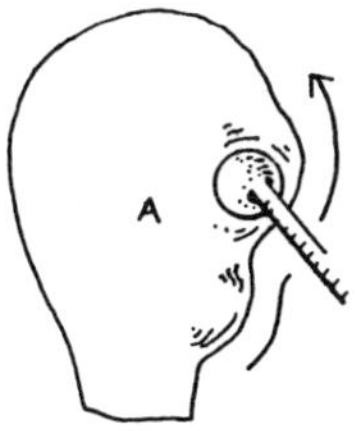

figure 2

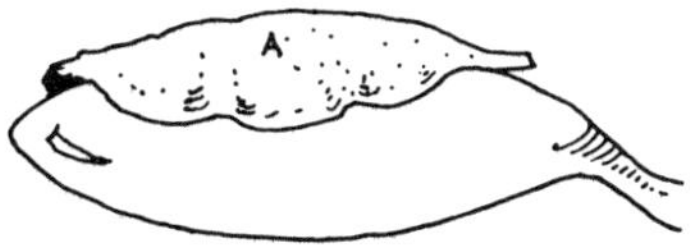

figure 3

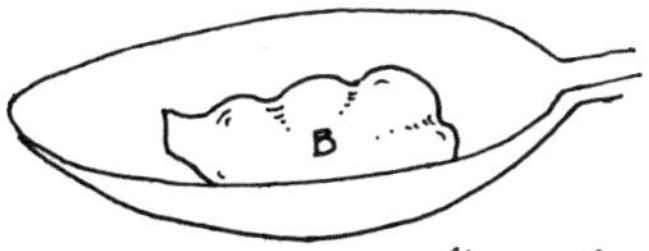

figure 4

figure 5

figure 6

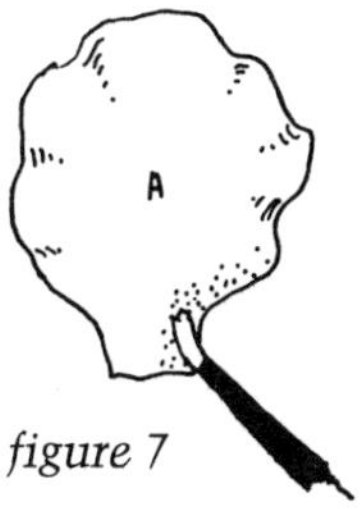

figure 7

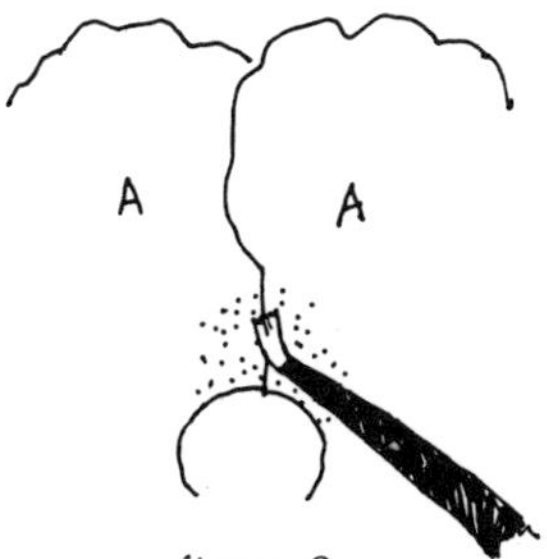

figure 8

figure 9

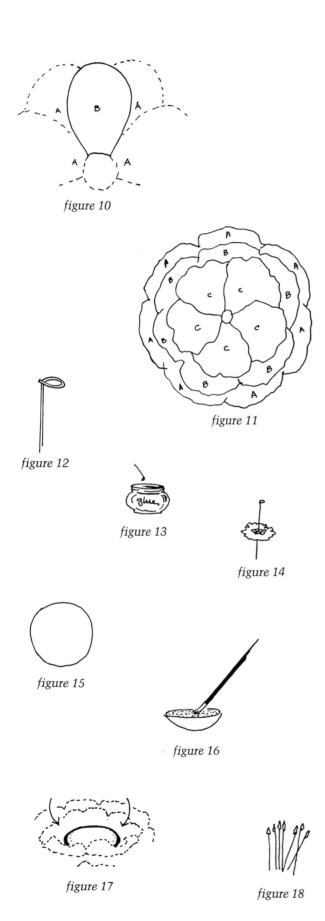

figure 10

figure 11

figure 12

figure 13

figure 14

figure 15

figure 16

figure 17

figure 18

Step 2. Cut out 6 petals slightly smaller than the 'A' petals. Repeat as in Step 1, this time placing each petal inside a dessert spoon. (These are the 'B' petals.) *See figure 4.*

Step 3. Cut out 5 more petals smaller than the 'B' petals. Repeat as in Step 2, this time placing each petal inside a teaspoon. (These are the 'C' petals.) *See figure 5.*

Step 4. Take the apple tray and make a large hole in its centre. *See figure 6.* Take the first petal from Step 1 and place it in the tray. Gum glue down the lower edge and place the next petal on top. *See figures 7, 8 and 9.* Continue until all petals are used or you have enough to fill the tray.

Step 5. Take the petals from Step 2 and paint gum glue on the base of the petals in the tray. Place the first 'B' petal in the centre of the lower petals. *See figure 10.* Repeat as in Step 4.

Step 6. Take the 'C' petals from Step 3 and, place them as described in Step 4. *See figure 11.*

Step 7. Take the wire and form the top into a circle. *See figure 12.* Dip the circle into gum glue, *see figure 13,* then push the wire through the centre of the petals. *See figure 14.*

Step 8. Make a small dome the size of a quarter (³/₄" or 2 cm). *See figure 15.* Paint the flat side with gum glue, *see figure 16,* and place on top of the wire. *See figure 17.* Take the very small yellow-headed stamens (approximately 36—each ⅛" in length), *see figure 18,* and place them at random in the dome. *See figure 19.* Lift up the sides of the petals and place tissue under the petals to allow them to dry. *See figure 20.* Let dry. Add calyx and rose hip. (For instructions on how to assemble calyxes and rose hips, refer to roses on page 29.)

Step 9. Dust and highlight the rose with food colour.

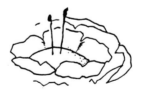

figure 19

figure 20

THE ROSE

Always a symbol of elegance, nobility and decorum, Roses have been cultivated for over 5,000 years. But Roses are much more ancient even than that, as fossils of rose plants millions of years old have been found in America, Europe and Asia. Today, there are more than 200 species in existence in temperate and subtropical regions of the northern hemisphere. Still the most popular flower of all, Roses look beautiful by themselves or in combination with Moth Orchids, Slipper Orchids, Carnations, Sweet Peas or Freesias accented with Rose Leaves.

Parts of the Flower

multi-petalled, calyx, hip, leaves

Tools and Materials

rose cutters
wire cutters
leaf cutters
24-gauge wire (for rose)
28-gauge wire (for leaves)
gum paste (in colour of choice)
white gum paste
moss green gum paste
gum glue
dusting colours
ball tool
spatula
rolling pin and board
cornstarch
white fat
X-acto knife

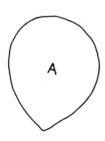

figure 1

figure 2

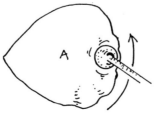

figure 3

figure 4

figure 5

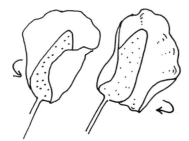

figure 6

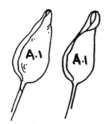

figure 7

figure 8

Method

Step 1. Make a hook at the end of the wire. *See figure 1.* Take a piece of gum paste, place it on the wire and shape it into a solid cone. *See figure 2.* Allow to dry.

Step 2. Prepare coloured gum paste in a deep shade for the first 3 petals, and progressively lighter colouring for each succeeding row of petals. To lighten, add half the quantity of white gum paste to the remaining coloured gum paste. (In other words, make each row of petals 50% lighter than the previous row.)
Roll out the gum paste very thinly, and cut out 3 petals in the darkest shade. *See figure 3.* Place each petal in the palm of your hand and, with the ball tool, thin around the top half. This will create a curling effect. (Do not thin the lower half.) *See figure 4.*

Step 3. Paint the cone with gum glue. *See figure 5.* Place the petal slightly above the cone by wrapping in the left side. Roll the petal around the cone to create a very tight bud. *See figure 6.* Slightly curl the tip of the petal. *See figure 7.*

Step 4. Repeat as above, only this time place the 2 petals ('A2' and 'A3') slightly higher than petal 'A1' and place opposite each other on the bud. *See figure 8.*

Step 5. Lighten the gum paste, roll out very thinly and cut out 2 more petals. Repeat as in Step 2, only this time place petals opposite each other and fold so that they overlap. Let dry.

figure 10

figure 9

figure 11

Step 6. Roll out gum paste, remembering to lighten once again. Cut out 3 more petals. For a large rose, repeat as above until desired size is achieved, remembering to lighten the paste for each row of petals. *See figure 9.*

Step 7. Take moss green paste and white paste and roll out each very thinly. Place the 2 colours together with the white paste on the top. Then, cut out the calyx. *See figure 10.* Make cuts at an angle into the centre of the calyx with an X-acto knife. *See figure 11.*

Step 8. Make a small rose hip. *See figure 12.* Gum glue the top and pull the wire through. *See figure 13.* Gum glue the centre of the calyx and attach to the rosehip and rose. *See figure 14.* Then pull the wire through the calyx to attach the white side to the flower. *See figure 15.*

Step 9. For instructions on how to make rose leaves, see page 64.

figure 12

figure 13

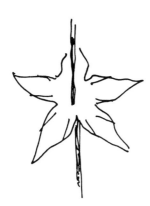

figure 14

figure 15

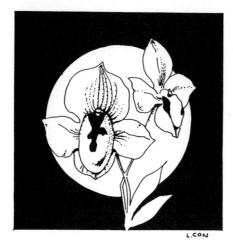

SLIPPER ORCHID
PAPHIOPEDILUM

The popular name for Paphiopedilum is "Lady's Slipper," derived from the curious pouch at the front of the flower which is composed of two petals joined together. The cupped formation resembles a slipper or small shoe. Originally from tropical Asia, these large, striking flowers come in many colours and variations of markings on the petals, the sepals and the pouches. Ideal as a main flower in arrangements, the Slipper Orchid looks beautiful when blended with Roses, accented with Ivy or with real Maidenhair Ferns.

Parts of the Flower

slipper, petals, sepals

Tools and Materials

slipper orchid cutters
wire cutter
24-gauge wire
gum paste
gum glue
dusting colours
ball tool
spatula
rolling pin and board
cornstarch
white fat
aluminum foil (shaped like a small open bowl)
Pam spray

Method

Step 1. Make a hook at the end of the wire. *See figure 1.* Attach a small piece of gum paste to the hooked end and shape as in *figure 2*. Let dry.

figure 1

figure 2

figure 3

figure 4

figure 5

figure 6

figure 7

figure 8

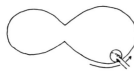

figure 9

figure 10

figure 11

Step 2. To Make Slipper:
Roll out gum paste thinly and cut out the slipper. *See figure 3.* Roll around the edges with the ball tool to thin them out without stretching or losing the shape. *See figure 4.* Paint the lower edge of the slipper with gum glue. *See figure 5.* Seam up the back of the slipper and turn the points under. Attach the bud between the folds. *See figure 6.* Place tissue under the slipper. *See figure 7.* Let dry.

Step 3. To Make Back Petals:
Roll out gum paste very thinly and cut out the back petals. *See figure 8.* To thin the edges, roll with the ball tool to create a slight curling effect. *See figure 9.* Fold the petal in half, lengthwise. *See figure 10.* Place the petal into the bowl-shaped foil. *See figure 11.* Set aside.

Step 4. To Make Sepals:
Roll out gum paste very thinly and cut out the sepals. *See figure 12.* Curl the edges as described in Step 3.

Step 5. To Attach Sepals and Petals:
Paint the narrow part of the back petals with gum glue. *See figure 13.* Place sepals across the lower petals. *See figure 14.* For illustration of petals in the foil, *See figure 15.*

Step 6. To Assemble Flower:
Paint the top petal with gum glue. *See figure 16.* Place the slipper part of the orchid through both petals and sepals. *See figure 17.* For side view, *see figure 18.*

Step 7. Lift up the slipper and shape petals with tissue and let dry.

Step 8. Take a small amount of paste. *See figure 19.* Shape into a heart. Paint the bud with gum glue and attach the heart over the bud. *See figure 20.* Let dry.

Step 9. Colour the flower and slipper as desired. To give the slipper a shiny look, spray with Pam.

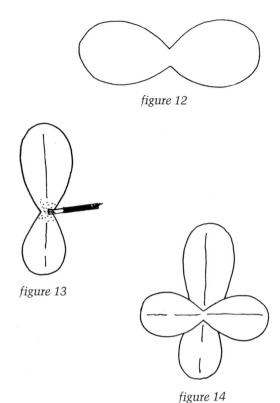

figure 12

figure 13

figure 14

figure 15

figure 16

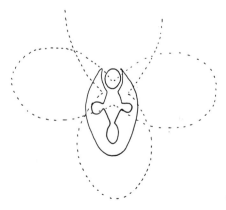

figure 17

figure 18

figure 19

figure 20

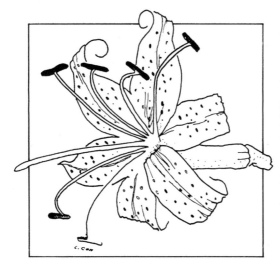

TIGER LILY
LILIUM TIGRINUM

Cultivated for their loveliness for over 3,000 years, Lilies have a cultural and symbolic significance in civilizations of the East and the West. The Tiger Lily, an exceptionally beautiful flower of this genus, was introduced in the West in 1804 from its native habitat in the Orient. It is most commonly orange in colour, plentifully dotted with purple-brown spots, but it can also be lemon yellow, white and/or pink. Excellent as a main flower in arrangements, Tiger Lilies look very attractive when combined with Roses and different-sized Rose leaves.

Parts of the Flower

6 petals, 6 stamens and 1 pistil

Tools and Materials

tiger lily cutter
wire cutters
26-gauge wire
28-gauge wire
gum paste
gum glue
dusting colours
ball tool
spatula
rolling pin and board
cornstarch
white fat
Royal icing, brown
aluminum foil, cone-shaped
veiner
food colour and/or non-toxic felt pen
cardboard tubing, 1" diameter

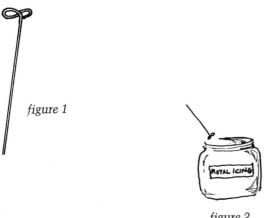

figure 1

figure 2

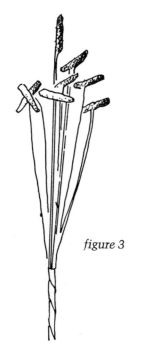

figure 3

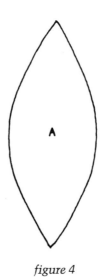

figure 4

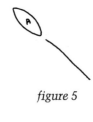

figure 5

Method

Step 1. Cut the 28-gauge wire into 6 pieces. Shape one end of each piece into a closed figure '8.' *See figure 1.* Dip the '8' into brown Royal icing. *See figure 2.* Let dry. These are the stamens. Take another length of wire, slightly longer than the other 6 pieces, and form a hook at one end. Dip the hook into brown Royal icing. Let dry. This is the pistil. Tape the stamens and pistils together so that the hooked wire (pistil) is slightly higher than the other 6 wires (stamens). *See figure 3.*

Step 2. Roll out the gum paste and cut out 3 of the largest petals. *See figure 4.* Thread the 26-gauge wire through the centre of the wire for approximately 1" taking care not to break through the paste. *See figure 5.* Roll around the edges with the ball tool. *See figure 6.* Then press the petal onto the veiner. *See figure 7.* To shape the petals, place each over cardboard tubing to dry. *See figure 8.* When dry, tape the 3 petals to the pistil-stamen assembly. *See figure 9.*

Step 3. Repeat Step 2, only this time cut 3 thin petals. Turn the flower upside down and instead of placing the petals onto a wire, gum glue down the undersides of the dried petals and attach the wet petals in between and behind the dry petals. *See figure 10.* While still holding the flower upside down, pack the undersides of wet petals with tissue and very gently place in cone-shaped aluminum foil to dry. Let dry.

Step 4. Dot all petals using either brown Royal icing, food colouring or a non-toxic felt pen. Dust the petals with colour.

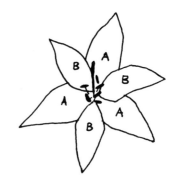

figure 10

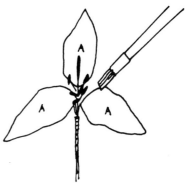

figure 9

figure 8

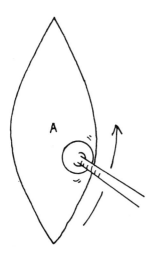

figure 6

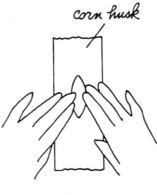

figure 7

SECONDARY FLOWERS

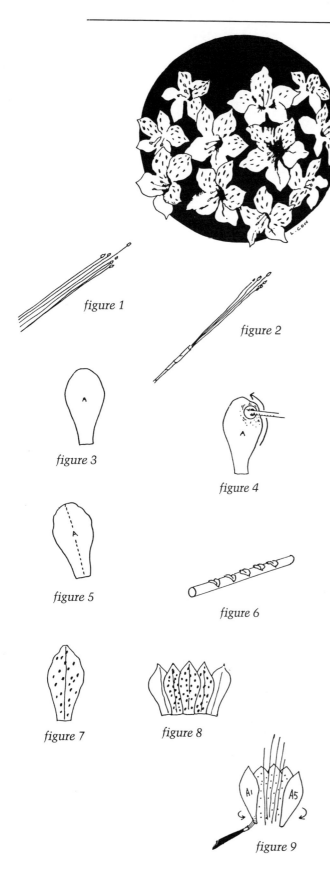

figure 1

figure 2

figure 3

figure 4

figure 5

figure 6

figure 7

figure 8

figure 9

AZALEA
AZALEA INDICA

Originally from China, these small evergreen shrubs with funnel-shaped flowers in clustered heads were introduced into Europe in 1810. They come in a tremendous range of colours including white, pink, salmon, crimson, magenta and orange. These flowers make an excellent main or secondary flower in arrangements.

Parts of the Flower

5 petals and stamens

Tools and Materials

azalea cutter
wire cutter
26-gauge wire
gum paste
gum glue
dusting colours
ball tool
spatula
rolling pin and board
cornstarch
white fat
wooden dowel
8 small-headed stamens
aluminum foil shaped into a cone (for drying the flower)

Method

Step 1. Take 8 stamens and group them together leaving one longer than the others. Tape the stamen grouping to 26-gauge wire. *See figures 1 and 2.*

Step 2. Roll out paste very thinly, and cut out 5 petals. *See figure 3.* Thin around the edges with a ball tool. *See figure 4.* Fold the petal in half and crease. *See figure 5.* Semi-dry over a wooden dowel. *See figure 6.*

Step 3. On one petal, paint dots. *See figure 7.* On two other petals, paint dots. *See figure 8.*

Step 4. Place the 3 dotted petals in the centre to form the top of the flower. Place the other two petals underneath.

Step 5. Wrap the petals around the wire and position the last 2 petals. *See figure 9.*

Step 6. Arrange the petals and place in foil cone to dry. Dust the centre middle petal with food colour and dust either side of the top outer petals with the same shade. Normally, the lower 2 petals are not dusted.

BOUGAINVILLEA
BOUGAINVILLEA GLABRA

Also known as Paper Flowers, these showy flowers, native to Brazil, were named after Louis Antoine de Bougainville who sailed around the world 1767-69. The small white flowers are surrounded most commonly by brilliant cerise bracts. The bracts also come in orange, lemon and pink varieties. Bougainvillea are particularly lovely when used as secondary flowers in arrangements with Roses, accented with Green Ivy.

Parts of the Flower

3 petals, 3 stamens

Tools and Materials

bougainvillea cutter
mini-forget-me-not cutter
wire cutters
30-gauge wire
28-gauge wire
gum paste
gum glue
dusting colours
ball tool
spatula
rolling pin and board
cornstarch
white fat
tweezers
corn husk

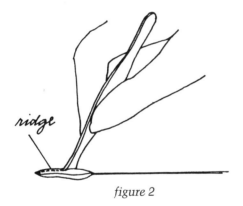

figure 1

ridge

figure 2

figure 3

figure 5

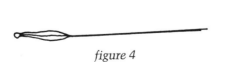

figure 4

figure 6

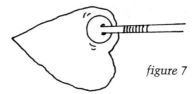

figure 7

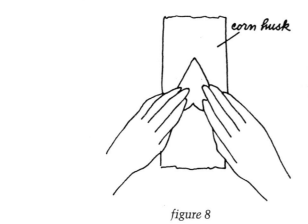

corn husk

figure 8

Method

Step 1. Cut the 30-gauge wire into 3 lengths, each approximately 3" (8 cm). Cover ¾" (2 cm) of the tip with a thin sausage of gum paste. *See figure 1.* With tweezers, pinch 5 ridges down the sides of the stamens. Shade the stamens to match the colour of the flower. *See figure 2.*

Step 2. For the first stamen, cut the tip into 5. Slightly hollow to create a hole. Colour the tip a soft cream-yellow shade. *See figure 3.* For the second stamen, make a mini-ball of gum paste and attach to the stamen. *See figure 4.* Dust with food colour. For the third stamen, cut out the mini-forget-me-not and gum glue to the tip of the third stamen. *See figure 5.* Ball tool the flower and make a small hole through the centre of the forget-me-not. Set aside to dry.

Step 3. Roll out gum paste very thinly and cut out 3 petals. *See figure 6.* With a ball tool, thin the edges. *See figure 7.* Vein the petal on the corn husk. *See figure 8.* Fold the petal in half, then gum glue the centre base of petal. *See figure 9.* Attach the dried stamens pinching the base of the petal. *See figure 10.* Shape the petal. Repeat for the other 2 petals. Join the petals together while they are still wet. *See figure 11.* Once the petals have completely dried, retape the flower together.

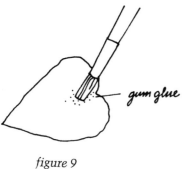

gum glue

figure 9

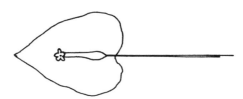

figure 10

figure 11

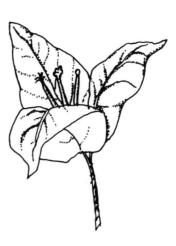

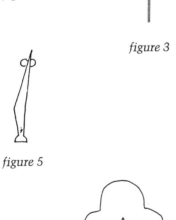

DENDROBIUM ORCHID

There are more than 1,000 species of this beautiful and varied genus, native to India, China, Japan, Australia and the South Pacific. The name is derived from the Greek *dendron* (tree) and *bios* (life). The flowers vary in size, colour and markings but are most commonly magenta or white with a magenta and yellow column. Dendrobium orchids make excellent secondary flowers in arrangements. Use three Orchids blended with Roses and/or Sweet Peas, accented with Ivy.

Parts of the Flower

column, throat, 2 petals, sepals

Tools and Materials

orchid cutters
wire cutter
24-gauge wire
gum paste
gum glue
dusting colours
ball tool
spatula
rolling pin and board
cornstarch
white fat
tweezers
apple tray
X-acto knife

figure 1

figure 2

figure 3

figure 4

figure 5

figure 6

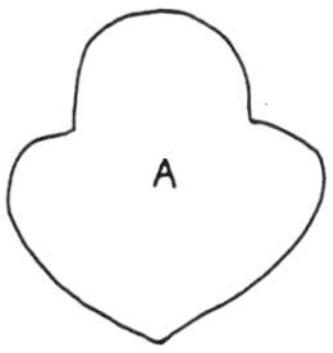

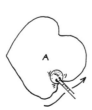

figure 8

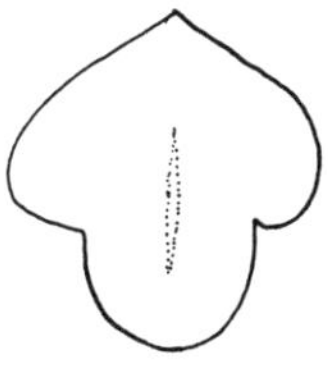

figure 10

figure 12

figure 7

figure 9

figure 11

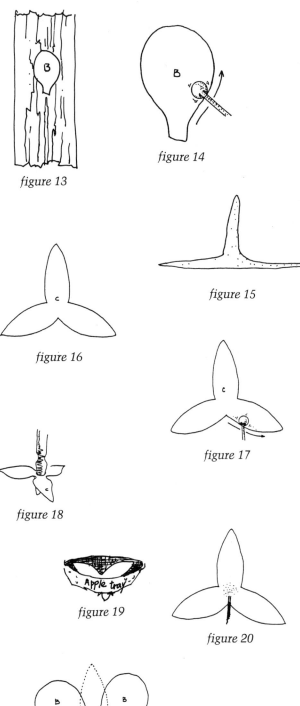

figure 13

figure 14

figure 15

figure 16

figure 17

figure 18

figure 19

figure 20

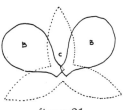

figure 21

figure 22

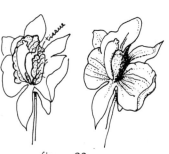

figure 23

Method

Step 1. To Make Column:
Note: The column of an orchid should never be longer than the distance from the bottom tip of the throat cutter to the first scallop.
Make a hook at the end of the wire. *See figure 1.* Place a small amount of gum paste on the wire tip to form a tapered column. Bend the tip of the column forward. *See figure 2.* Slightly hollow the underside while creating a hump at the top end. *See figure 3.* Take a very tiny piece of gum paste, the same size as shown in *figure 4* and mark the centre with the X-acto knife. *See figure 5.* Paint with gum glue. *See figure 6.* Attach to the tip of the column. *See figure 7.* (This piece is always left white.) Let dry.

Step 2. To Make Throat:
Roll out gum paste very thinly and cut out the throat. *See figure 8.* Thin around the edges with the ball tool. (Do not curl.) *See figure 9.* Take tweezers and pinch the centre of the throat. *See figure 10.* Paint the sides and the base of the column with gum glue and attach the throat. *See figure 11.* Let dry.

Step 3. To Make Petals:
Cut out 2 'B' petals. *See figure 12.* Vein the petals. *See figure 13.* Thin around the edge with the ball tool, taking care not to curl the petals. *See figure 14.* Set aside.

Step 4. To Make Sepals:
Cut out sepals "Mexican Hat" style. *See figures 15 and 16.* Thin around the edges with the ball tool. *See figure 17.* Hollow out the centre of the sepal. *See figure 18.* Place the sepal in the apple tray. *See figure 19.* Paint the centre with gum glue. *See figure 20.*

Step 5. To Finish Flower:
Place 'B' petals as shown in *figure 21.* Pull the wire through the petals and sepals. *See figure 22.* For side view, *see figure 23.* Taking care not to break the hump from the back sepals, pack with tissue and let dry.

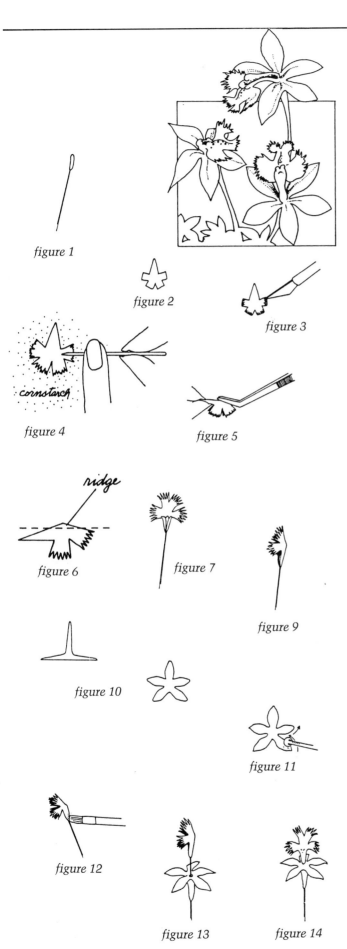

figure 1

figure 2

figure 3

figure 4

cornstarch

figure 5

ridge

figure 6

figure 7

figure 9

figure 10

figure 11

figure 12

figure 13

figure 14

EPIDENDRUM ORCHID

Native to tropical and subtropical America, this dainty flower is also known as the Poor Man's Orchid, Crucifix Orchid or Baby Orchid. It comes in many shades of red, pink, orange, yellow, white and mauve and makes an excellent secondary flower in arrangements with Roses or Moth Orchids accented with Variegated Ivy. It can also look very attractive when combined with Sweet Peas.

Parts of the Flower

throat, column, back 5 petals

Tools and Materials

epidendrum orchid cutters	spatula
wire cutter	rolling pin and board
28-gauge wire	cornstarch
gum paste	white fat
gum glue	round wooden toothpick
dusting colours	tweezers
ball tool	X-acto knife

Method

Step 1. To Make Column:
Note: The column of an orchid should never be longer than the distance from the bottom tip of the throat cutter to the first scallop.
With a 28-gauge wire, roll a very small piece of paste onto the end of the wire. *See figure 1.* It should be no longer than the length of the top section of the cutter.

Step 2. To Make Throat:
Roll out the gum paste thinly and cut out the labellum (or throat). *See figure 2.* With an X-acto knife, make small cuts into the arms and legs of the throat. *See figure 3.* With a round wooden toothpick, frill the cut edges. *See figure 4.*

Step 3. With a pair of tweezers make a ridge from the base of the arms to the top of the legs. *See figures 5 and 6.*

Step 4. Gum glue the column very lightly and place the column in the centre top half of the throat. *See figure 7.* Press the 2 sides together to enclose the column. *See figure 9.* Cut off any excess paste and smooth the seam. Set aside to dry.

Step 5. Roll out paste "Mexican Hat" method, making a very thin stem. *See figure 10.* Cut out the back petals. *See figure 11.* With a ball tool, thin the edges of the petals. *See figure 12.* Gum glue the base of the dried column. *See figure 13.* Thread the wire through the centre of the petals, making sure it goes through the stem of the Mexican Hat. *See figure 14.*

FREESIA
FREESIA REFRACTA

Native to South Africa, these dainty members of the Iris family were introduced in Europe around 1875. They grow in a wide range of brilliant colours including white, yellow, mauve, pink, red and violet. The showy flowers, popular as secondary flowers in bridal arrangements, are borne on high arching stems. Freesia look beautiful blended with Roses and accented with Rose leaves or Variegated Ivy. They are also very attractive when combined with Irises or other main flowers. Because it is so time-consuming to create a completed stem with its eleven or so buds and flowers in varying stages, my preference is to use single open flowers as secondary flowers in arrangements.

Parts of the Flower

6-petal, trumpeted flowers with calyx

Tools and Materials

freesia cutter
hyacinth cutter for calyx
wire cutters
28-gauge wire (for buds)
26-gauge wire (for main stem)
gum paste
gum glue
dusting colours
ball tool
spatula
rolling pin and board
cornstarch
white fat
scissors
white, headless stamens

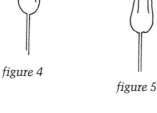

figure 1

figure 2

figure 3

figure 4

figure 5

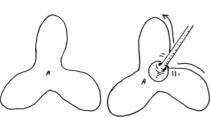

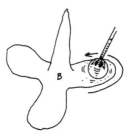

figure 8

figure 6

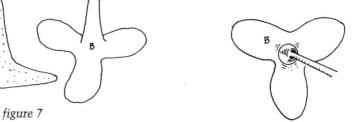

figure 7

figure 9

Method

Step 1. Tape 5 headless stamens together on 24-gauge wire. *See figure 1.* Set aside.

Step 2. To Make Small Dark Green Bud:
Make a small hook at the end of the 28-gauge wire and place a small piece of dark green gum paste on the hook. Shape as shown in *figure 2.* With scissors, make 2 small cuts. *See figure 3.* Let dry.

Step 3. To Make Slightly Larger Bud:
Repeat, only this time mix half of the colour of the flower into the paste to create a marbled effect and make the bud slightly larger than in Step 2. *See figure 4.* Let dry.

Step 4. To Make Largest Bud:
Repeat as above, making the bud larger again and in the solid colour of the flower. *See figure 5.* Let dry.

Step 5. To Make Petals:
Roll out the gum paste very thinly and cut out petal 'A.' With the ball tool, thin around the edges. *See figure 6.* Cut out petal 'B' using the "Mexican Hat" method. *See figure 7.* Thin around the edges of petal 'B' with the ball tool. *See figure 8.* Holding petal 'B,' slightly hollow the centre. *See figure 9.* With gum glue, paint the centre. *See figure 10.* Attach Petal 'A' to petal 'B.' *See figure 11.* Pull the stamens (from Step 1) through the centre of the flower. *See figure 12.* At the same time, create a long trumpet. Pack the centre of the flower with tissue to shape. *See figure 13.* Let dry.

Step 6. To Make Calyx:
Roll out dark green gum paste using the Hyacinth cutter. *See figure 14.* Cut 3 calyxes from one cutter. *See figure 15.* Thin around the edges with a ball tool. *See figure 16.* Gum glue the calyx and attach to the base of the buds and flowers. *See figure 17.* Let dry.

Step 7. To Assemble:
Attach the smallest buds first and add each gradation in size from the smallest bud to the completed open flowers. *See figure 18.*

figure 17

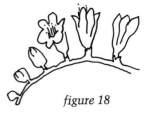

figure 18

figure 16

figure 15

figure 14

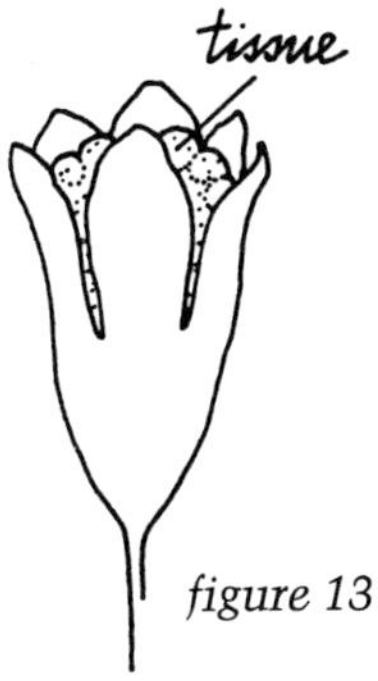

figure 13

figure 12

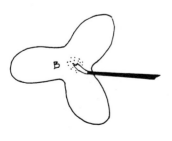

figure 10

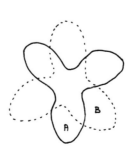

figure 11

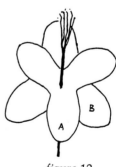

GARDEN PANSY
VIOLA X WITTROCKIANA

These familiar, variously coloured garden flowers are very pretty with their large, prominently marked petals. They are ideal as secondary flowers in arrangements with any other garden flowers such as Roses, Sweet Peas or Carnations.

Parts of the Flower

calyx, 5 irregular petals

Tools and Materials

pansy cutters
calyx cutter
wire cutter
26-gauge wire
gum paste
green gum paste for calyx
gum glue
dusting colours
ball tool
spatula
rolling pin and board
cornstarch
white fat
scissors
round toothpick

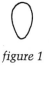

figure 1

figure 2

figure 3

figure 4

figure 5

figure 6

figure 7

figure 8

figure 9

Method

Step 1. To Make Calyx:
Make up a small amount of green gum paste for the calyx. Roll the gum paste into a teardrop. *See figure 1.* Cut the rounded part of the teardrop into 5. *See figure 2.*

Step 2. Open out the 5 petals, *See figure 3,* and with a round toothpick hold the petal over your finger. *See figure 4.* Roll the stick back and forth over the petals. *See figure 5.* This both stretches and thins them.

Step 3. Make a small hook at the end of the wire. Dip the hook into the gum glue and pull through the centre of the calyx. *See figure 6.* Let dry.

Step 4. To Make Top Petals:
Roll out gum paste very thinly and cut out the top 2 petals. *See figure 7.* Thin around the edges with a ball tool. *See figure 8.* Gum glue the bases on the backs of the petals and place into the dry calyx. Place the top left-hand petal first, *See figure 9,* and overlap the right-hand petal. *See figure 10.*

Step 5. To Make Side Petals:
Repeat Step 4, this time cutting out the 2 side petals. Thin around the petals and gum glue into position. *See figure 11.*

Step 6. To Make Skirt:
Cut out the skirt of the pansy. *See figure 12.* Instead of ball tooling the edges, lightly ruffle with a toothpick. *See figure 13.* Gum glue the top and place on top of the other petals. *See figure 14.*

Step 7. To Decorate:
Pipe a small yellow dot into the centre of the flower. *See figure 15.* Paint the markings typical to a pansy. *See figure 16.* Dust the whole flower. Let dry.

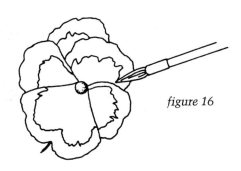

figure 16

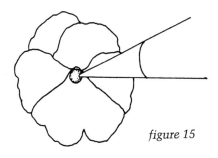

figure 15

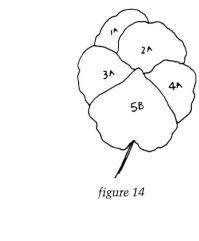

figure 14

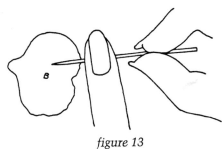

figure 12

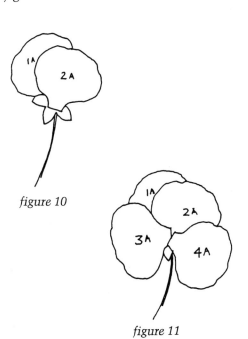

figure 10

figure 11

figure 13

GLADIOLUS
GLADIOLUS X GUADAVENSIS, HYBRIDS

Native to Europe, the Mediterranean region, the Near East and tropical and southern Africa, Gladiola (from the Latin diminutive of *gladius*, sword, referring to the foliage) vary from the small dainty, indigenous species to the more commonly known tall, magnificent hybrid varieties. Often bicoloured, they come in a wide array of colours, from white and yellow to pink, salmon, orange, crimson, red, mauve and purple. As Gladiola are such large flowers (3½ to 4½ feet high), single blooms can be used as secondary flowers with Roses and accented with different-sized Rose Leaves.

Parts of the Flower

sheath, buds, 6-petalled open flower, 2-petalled semi-open

Tools and Materials

gladiolus cutter
wire cutters
28-gauge wire (for the stamens)
24-gauge wire (for the buds)
ball tool
gum paste
gum glue
dusting colours
spatula
rolling pin and board
cornstarch
white fat
wooden stick
wooden dowel
white tape
white stamens, without heads
veining tool such as dried corn husk
aluminum foil shaped in a cone

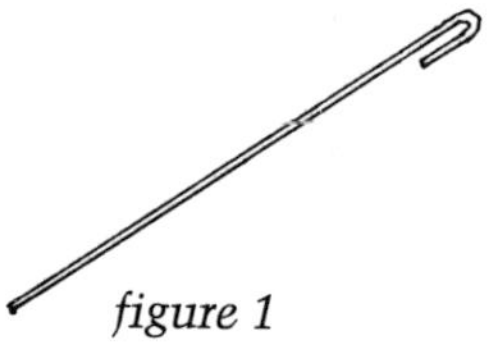

figure 1

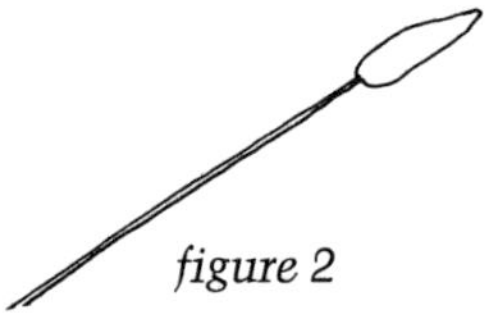

figure 2

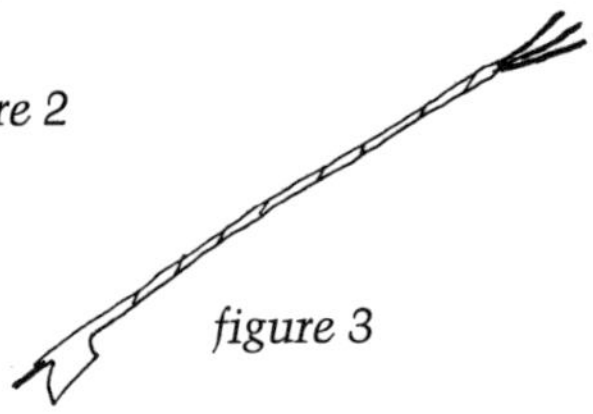

figure 3

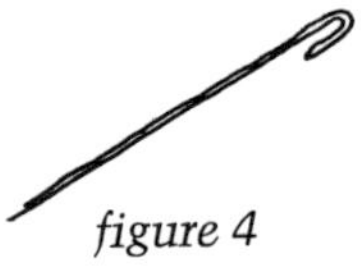

figure 4

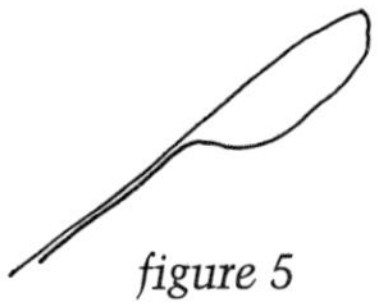

figure 5

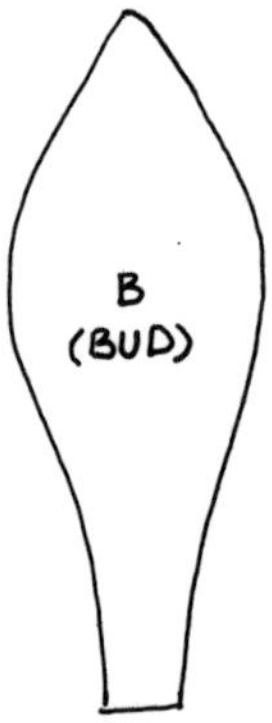

figure 6

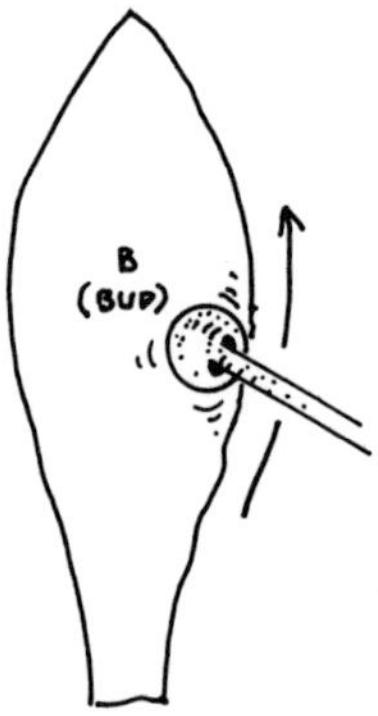

B (BUD)

figure 7

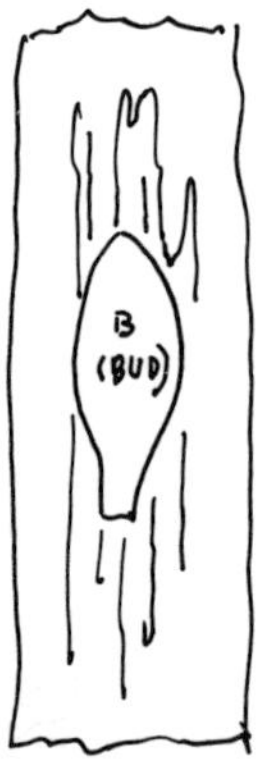

B (BUD)

figure 8

B (BUD)

figure 9

figure 10

Method

Step 1. Cover the 28-gauge wire with white tape and cut wire into 5 pieces. Make a small hook at the end of 3 of the pieces. *See figure 1.* Take a very small amount of white gum paste and mold over the hook. *See figure 2.* (Repeat for other 2 pieces.) Let dry.

Step 2. Take the 4th piece of wire and 3 white stamens. Remove the heads from the stamens. Tape together. *See figure 3.* Let dry. Set aside. Tape results of Step 1 and Step 2 together, leaving Step 2 stamens slightly longer.

Step 3. To Make Bud:
Take the 24-gauge wire and make a hook at the end. *See figure 4.* Place gum paste over the hooked wire and shape into a straight-edged crescent. *See figure 5.* Let dry. Roll out green gum paste thinly and cut out one sheath (petal 'B'). *See figure 6.* Thin around the edges. *See figure 7.* Vein by placing bud on veining tool. *See figure 8.* Paint the bud with gum glue. *See figure 9.* Place the bud in the centre of the sheath. *See figure 10.* Wrap the sheath around the bud. *See figure 11.*

Step 4. Repeat Step 3, only this time, cut petal 'C' (sheath) and place the seamed bud in the centre of petal 'C.' *See figure 12.* Wrap the sheath around the bud onto the wire, covering the wire with the green sheath.

Step 5. Repeat Steps 3 and 4 for extra buds and attach to the sides of the wire (not to the back of the wire). *See figure 13.* Let dry. The buds should be attached so they appear to grow from the sides of the wire as is the case with the real flower.

Step 6. To Make Semi-Open Flower:
Roll out the gum paste very thinly and cut out one of petal 'D.' *See figure 14.* Ruffle around the edges with a wooden stick and pleat together. *See figure 15.* Cut out petal 'B.' *See figure 16.* Place the dried pleated petal into petal 'B.' *See figure 17.* Repeat Step 4 for the sheath, attaching the semi-open flower to the main stem. *See figure 18.* Let dry.

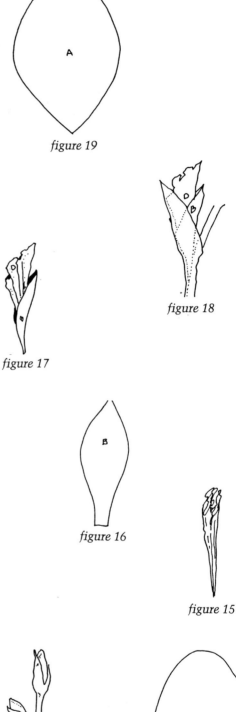

figure 19

figure 18

figure 17

figure 16

figure 15

figure 11

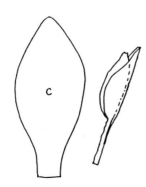

figure 12

figure 13

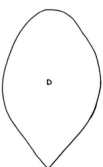

figure 14

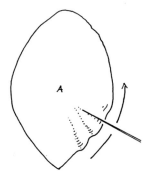

figure 20

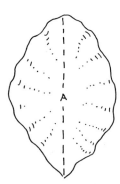

figure 21

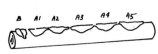

figure 22

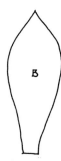

figure 23

Step 7. To Make Open Flower:
Roll out gum paste very thinly and cut out 5 of petal 'A.' *See figure 19.* Place the petal on the table and, with the wooden stick, roll around the edges of the petal. *See figure 20.* Fold the petal in half lengthwise. *See figure 21.* Place the 5 petals lengthwise on a wooden dowel and allow to semi-dry. *See figure 22.* Roll out gum paste very thinly and cut out petal 'B.' *See figure 23.* Proceed as above except allow the petal to dry completely on the wooden dowel. *See figure 22.*

Step 8. To Assemble Open Flower:
Take 3 large petals 'A' and paint the base of each with gum glue. *See figure 24.* Arrange the petals to form a triangle around the taped stamens, as shown in *figure 3*, placing petals 1, 2 and 3 as in *figure 25.* Place petals 4 and 5 at the top and arrange petals 4 and 5 as shown in *figure 26.* Lastly, place petal 'B' as in *figure 27.* Place the flower into the cone-shaped aluminum foil, placing tissue underneath the petals as required to give a realistic look. Let dry.

Step 9. Repeat Step 6, attaching the sheath to the flower and main stem. Highlight the flowers with dusting colours.

figure 25

figure 26

figure 24

figure 27

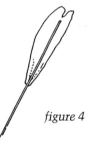

MINI-BEARDED IRIS
IRIS GERMANICA

Cultivated for centuries, these attractive flowers, named for Iris, the Greek goddess of the rainbow, come in many shades from white, pink, red, yellow, bronze and tan, to violet, mauve, purple and pale blue. Popularly known as Flags, they are characterized by prominent gold beards at the top inside of the falls.

Parts of the Flower

3 vertical petals (standards) alternating with 3 drooping petals (falls)

Tools and Materials

iris cutters (Note: For a full-sized Iris, "B-2" petals require a cutter of a different shape.)
wire cutters
28-gauge wire
24-gauge wire
gum paste
gum glue
ball tool
spatula
rolling pin and board
cornstarch
white fat
yellow-coloured sugar
Royal icing bag with a #1 tip

figure 1

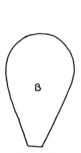

figure 2

figure 3

figure 5

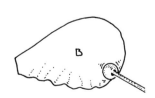

figure 4

figure 7

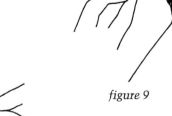

figure 9

figure 6

figure 8

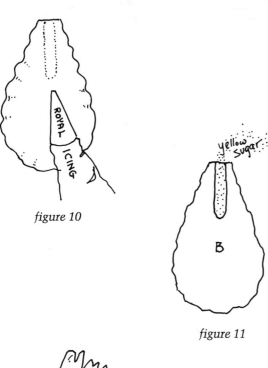

figure 10

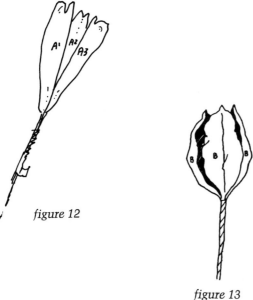

figure 11

figure 12

figure 13

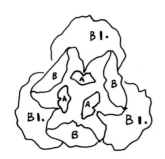

figure 14

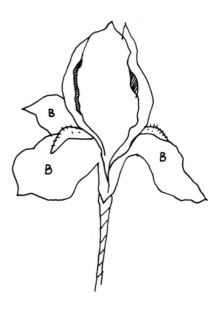

Method

Step 1. Roll out gum paste very thinly and cut out 3 pistils 'A.' *See figure 1.* Thin around the edges. *See figure 2.* Fold pistils in half to shape. *See figure 3.* Take 28-gauge wire and dip into gum glue. Place the wire on the backs of the pistils. *See figure 4.* Let dry.

Step 2. Roll out gum paste thinly, and cut out 3 petals 'B.' *See figure 5.* With the ball tool, thin the edges of the petals. *See figure 6.* Thread the wire through the cente of the petals taking care that the wire does not break through. *See figure 7.* Shape these petals ('B') up and over toward you to give the effect of a semi-open cup. *See figure 8.* Let dry.

Step 3. Repeat Step 2, only do not ruffle the lower petals as much as the top 3 petals. This time, shape the petals 'B-1' down and out. *See figure 9.* Let dry.

Step 4. Take the Royal icing and, starting at the centre of the inside base of petal 'B,' with the #1 tip, pipe approximately ¼ of the way along the length of the petal. *See figure 10.* Repeat for other 'B' petals. Sprinkle the yellow sugar on the wet Royal icing. This creates the pollen look on the petals. *See figure 11.* Let dry. Repeat for other 2 'B' petals and on the outside of petals 'B-1.' Let dry.

Step 5. To assemble, take the 3 pistils and tape together. *See figure 12.* Take the 3 outer 'B' petals and tape to the pistils. *See figure 13.* Repeat for the 3 lower petals, alternating petals so that the lower petal is placed between the opening of the top 3 petals. *See figure 14.*

OX-EYE DAISY
CASTALIS NUDICAULIS

These very pretty yellow-centred white flowers, native to Europe and Britain, are very attractive in arrangements for garden weddings either as a main or as a secondary flower.

Parts of the Flower

multi-petalled

Tools and Materials

daisy cutter
wire cutter
28-gauge wire
gum paste
gum glue
dusting colours
ball tool
spatula
rolling pin and board
cornstarch
white fat
wooden stick
small piece of tulle

Method

Step 1. Cut out petal. *See figure 1.* With the wooden stick, press the centre of each petal across your finger to mark the petals. *See figure 2.*

Step 2. Slightly hollow the centre of the flower. *See figure 3.* Paint the centre with gum glue. *See figure 4.* Shape the end of the wire into a loop *See figure 5.* Pull through the centre of the flower. *See figure 6.*

Step 3. Take a small piece of yellow gum paste and shape into a sightly raised dome. Press the paste over the tulle. *See figure 7.* Gum glue the centre of the flower (with wire attached) and place the dome over the wire. *See figure 8.* Let dry.

figure 1

figure 2

figure 3

figure 4

figure 5

figure 7

figure 8

figure 6

PERUVIAN LILY
ALSTROEMERIA

Also known as Chilean Lady, Flower of the Incas and New Zealand Christmas Bell, this pretty flower, a native of Chile, comes in many colours including white, yellow, pink, pale green and various shades of red and purple. Very popular with brides, it can be used as a secondary flower with Roses, accented with Green Ivy.

Parts of the Flower

6 petals and 6 stamens

Tools and Materials

Peruvian lily cutter
wire cutters
26-gauge wire
gum paste
gum glue
dusting colours
ball tool
spatula
rolling pin and board
cornstarch
white fat
scissors
6 yellow-green stamens (for the yellow flower)
6 burgundy stamens (for the pink flower)
white tape (for the yellow flower)
pink tape (for the pink flower)

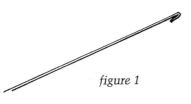

figure 1

figure 2

figure 3

figure 4

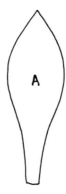

figure 5

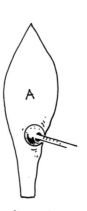

figure 6

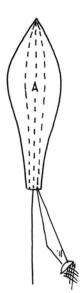

figure 7

Method

Step 1. Make a small hook at the end of the wire. *See figure 1.* Place a very small piece of gum paste on the hooked end of the wire and flatten into an oval shape. *See figure 2.* With scissors, make marks down the sides to form indentations on the stamens. *See figures 3 and 4.* Repeat 5 more times. Six stamens are required for each flower. Let dry.

Step 2. Roll out gum paste thinly, and cut out 3 petals 'A.' *See figure 5.* Thin around the edges with the ball tool. *See figure 6.* Thread the wire through the petals and shape as desired. With X-acto knife, mark petals as shown in *figure 7.* Let dry.

Step 3. Repeat Step 2, except use larger cutter 'B.' *See figure 8.* Using a ball tool, thin around the edges and slightly widen the petals. *See figure 9.* Thread the wire through the petals and mark with the X-acto knife. *See figure 10.* Shape the petals as desired and let dry.

Step 4. Mark the 3 inside petals 'A' with a non-toxic felt tip pen. Two petals should be marked as in *figure 11,* and the third petal should be marked as in *figure 12.*

Step 5. Tape the stamens together in uneven lengths. *See figure 13.* Place the 2 petals, *figure 11,* at the top of the stamens, and place 1 petal, *figure 12,* at the base. Tape together. *See figure 14.* Take outer 3 petals, *figure 10,* and place and tape as shown in *figure 15.* To achieve a natural look, refer to a fresh flower and dust in the colour of your choice.

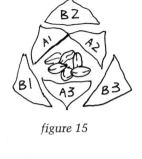

figure 15

figure 14

figure 13

figure 12

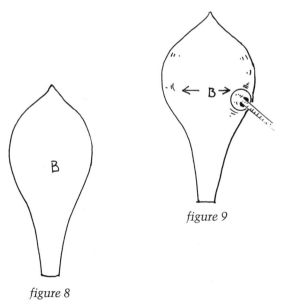

figure 9

figure 8

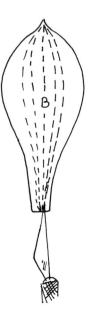

figure 10

figure 11

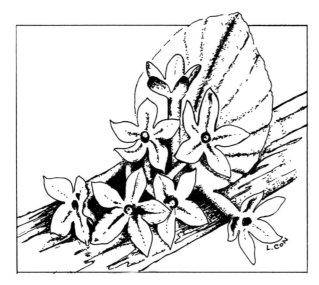

STEPHANOTIS
ASCLEPIADACEA

Also known as the Madagascar Chaplet, Floradora or Malagasy Jasmine Wax Flower, these sweetly scented tubular white bells with flaring petals are extremely popular as secondary flowers in bridal arrangements, wedding bouquets and corsages.

Parts of the Flower

5-petal calyx, trumpet-style flower

Tools and Materials

stephanotis cutter
wire cutter
28-gauge wire
gum paste
gum glue
dusting colours, soft yellow or pink
ball tool
spatula
rolling pin and board
cornstarch
white fat
wooden stick
small scissors

Method

Step 1. Make a bulb at the end of the paste and roll it out using the "Mexican Hat" method. Cut out the flower and hollow out the centre. *See figures 1 and 2.*

Step 2. Hook the wire and dip it into the gum glue. *See figures 3 and 4.* Pull the wire through the centre of the flower. *See figures 5 and 6.*

Step 3. Roll the flower back and forth between your fingers to lengthen the trumpet. *See figure 7.* (This flower is similar to the bouvardia in that both have long trumpets.) With a small pair of scissors, cut the 5-petal calyx at the base of the flower. Let dry.

Step 4. Dust the hollow centre of the flower with soft yellow or pink colouring. To achieve the waxy sheen that is natural to this flower, steam over a boiling kettle.

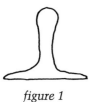

figure 1

figure 2

figure 3

gum glue

figure 4

figure 5

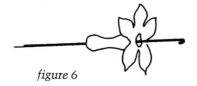

figure 6

figure 7

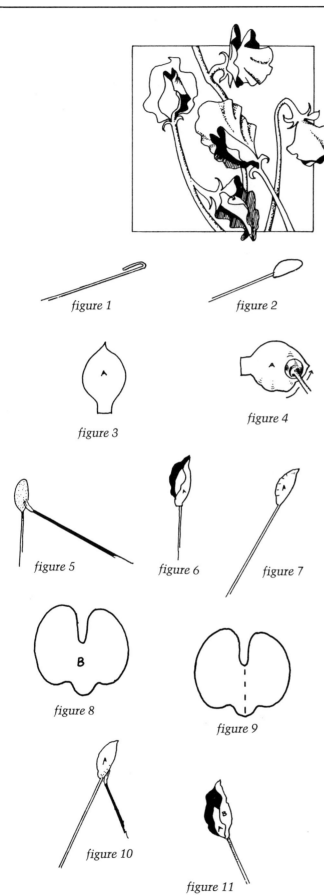

figure 1

figure 2

figure 3

figure 4

figure 5

figure 6

figure 7

figure 8

figure 9

figure 10

figure 11

figure 12

figure 13

SWEET PEA
LATHYRUS ODORATUS

Originally from Sicily and introduced in 1700, these well-loved, familiar flowers are shapely, fragrant and undoubtedly beautiful. Colours vary from white, yellow, pink, red and crimson to mauve and purple. They are excellent as secondary flowers in arrangements with Roses as a main flower, accented with Variegated Ivy.

Parts of the Flower

dual petal, pea pod calyx, tendrils, leaves

Tools and Materials

sweet pea cutters
calyx cutter
leaf cutter
wire cutter
32-gauge wire (for tendrils)
28-gauge wire (for leaves)
26-gauge wire (for flowers)
gum paste
gum glue
dusting colours
ball tool
spatula
rolling pin and board
cornstarch
white fat
wooden stick

Method

Step 1. To Make Pea Pod:
With the 26-gauge wire, form a hook. *See figure 1.* Attach a small piece of gum paste to the hooked wire and form it into a crescent shape. *See figure 2.* Let dry.

Step 2. To Make Petal 'A':
Roll out gum paste very thinly, and cut out petal 'A.' *See figure 3.* Thin around the edges with a ball tool. *See figure 4.* Paint the pod with gum glue. *See figure 5.* Attach the petal, seaming it at the crescent. *See figures 6 and 7.* Let dry.

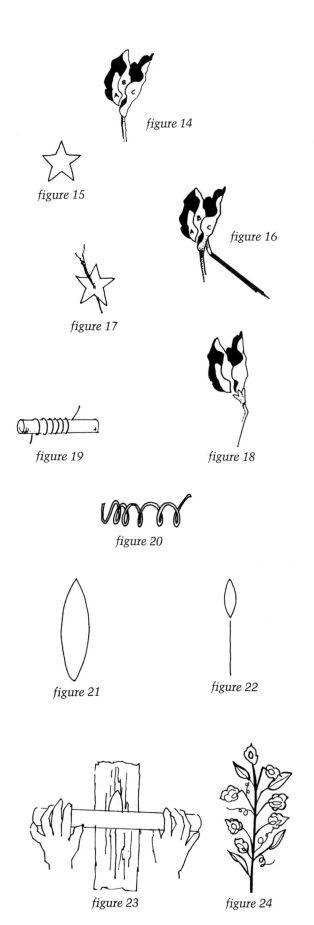

figure 14

figure 15

figure 16

figure 17

figure 19

figure 18

figure 20

figure 21

figure 22

figure 23

figure 24

Step 3. To Make Petal 'B':
Roll out gum paste very thinly, and cut out petal 'B.' *See figure 8.* Thin around the edges with a ball tool, slightly curling the edges. Then fold the petal in half, towards you. *See figure 9.* Paint the base of the pod with gum glue. *See figure 10.* Attach petal 'B' to the base of the pod. *See figure 11.*

Step 4. Repeat Step 3, this time using cutter for petal 'C.' *See figure 12.* Paint the base of the flower with gum glue. *See figure 13.* Attach petal 'C' ensuring that the petal is pulled slightly away from the top of the open flower. *See figure 14.* Let dry.

Step 5. To Make Calyx:
Roll out green gum paste very thinly and cut out calyx. *See figure 15.* Paint base of the flower with gum glue. *See figure 16.* Thread the wire through the calyx. *See figure 17.* Attach the calyx to the base of the flower. *See figure 18.*

Step 6. To Make Tendrils:
Take 32-gauge covered wire and wrap it around the wooden stick. *See figure 19.* Slide the wrapped wire off the stick and open slightly. *See figure 20.*

Step 7. To Make Leaves:
Roll out green gum paste very thinly and cut out leaves. *See figure 21.* Thread 28-gauge wire through centre of the leaf, taking care that the wire does not break through the leaf. *See figure 22.* Vein the leaf. *See figure 23.* Shape the leaf and allow to dry.

Step 8. To Assemble Flower:
To assemble, slightly bend the flower just below the calyx and attach up to 7 flowers on a wire, with the tendrils and leaves. *See figure 24.*

FILLER FLOWERS

BOUVARDIA
BOUVARDIA LONGIFLORA

Named after Dr. Charles Bouvard (1572-1658), these delicate, white, 4-lobed flowers, native to Mexico, resemble jasmine. Bouvardia are excellent as filler flowers in bridal arrangements and look particularly beautiful with Roses, Sweet Peas and Orchids. For greenery, use Ivy leaves.

Parts of the Flower

4 petals with a long trumpet

Tools and Materials

30-gauge wire
gum paste
gum glue
dusting colours
ball tool
spatula
rolling pin and board
cornstarch
white fat
wooden stick to hollow out the flower
small-pointed scissors

(This is one flower that can be made very easily without a cutter, a real advantage if you need to make a lot of them in a hurry. The flower is molded instead of cut.)

Method

Step 1. Take a very small piece of white paste and roll it into a very long tear drop. *See figure 1.*

Step 2. Cut the rounded part of the tear drop into 4. *See figure 2.*

Step 3. Open out the 4 petals and, with the wooden stick, *See figure 3*, hold the petal over your finger and roll the stick back and forth over the petals. This both stretches and thins the petal. *See figure 4.*

Step 4. Make a very small hook at the end of the wire. Dip the head of the wire into the gum glue and pull through the centre of the flower. *See figure 5.* Let dry.

figure 1

figure 2

figure 3

figure 4

figure 5

ENGLISH PRIMROSE
PRIMULA VULGARIS HYBRID

Also known as Polyanthus, these attractive blooms, a cross between Primrose and Cowslips, are originally from Southern and Western Europe. They come in many colours including white, pale yellow, pink, red and various shades of blue and violet. Excellent as fillers in arrangements for garden weddings, English Primroses look lovely when combined with Roses and Sweet Peas, accented with Variegated Ivy.

Parts of the Flower

4 petals

Tools and Materials

primrose cutter
wire cutter
28-gauge wire
gum paste
gum glue
dusting colours
very small ball tool
spatula
rolling pin and board
cornstarch
white fat
small piece foam
X-acto knife
wooden stick

Method

Step 1. Roll out paste "Mexican Hat" method. *See figure 1.* Cut out the flower. *See figure 2.* Place the top of the flower onto the foam. Rotate the small ball tool around the edges of the petal. *See figure 3.*

Step 2. While holding the flower, mark each petal with a knife. *See figure 4.* Slightly hollow the centre of the flower with the wooden stick. *See figure 5.*

Step 3. Make a small hook on the wire. *See figure 6.* Dip the hook into the gum glue. *See figure 7.* Pull the wire through the centre of the primrose. *See figure 8.* Let dry.

Step 4. Dust the centre of the flower with either a soft yellow or any of the colours mentioned above.

figure 1

figure 2

figure 3

figure 4

figure 5

figure 6

figure 7

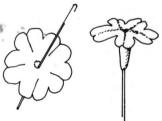

figure 8

FORGET-ME-NOT
MYOSOTIS SCROPIOIDES

Native to Europe and Asia, these tiny flowers are most commonly a clear sky-blue with a yellow, pink or white 'eye.' They also grow in many other shades of blue from deep to pale and in pink, white and yellow. As they usually grow in clusters, they can be grouped together and used as a filler flower to compliment Roses, Sweet Peas, Carnations or any other garden flowers. Excellent in arrangements for garden weddings, they also look splendid when combined with Lilacs and Lily of the Valley.

Parts of the Flower

5 petals and stamens

Tools and Materials

forget-me-not cutter
wire cutter
small piece of foam
gum paste
gum glue
dusting colours
small ball tool
spatula
rolling pin and board
cornstarch
white fat
very small-headed yellow stamens

Method

Step 1. Roll gum paste very thinly. Cut out flowers. *See figure 1.* Place on the foam. (Do not cut more than 6 flowers at a time as they dry quickly and you will not have time to shape them.)

Step 2. With the small ball tool, stroke the petals inwards towards the centre of the flower to create a cupped effect. *See figure 2.*

Step 3. Take the small-headed stamens and dip the head only into the gum glue. *See figure 3.* Then thread the stamens through the flower so the head is in the centre of the cup. *See figure 4.*

Step 4. Allow to dry, then group together in bunches of 3 or 5 flowers. *See figure 5.*

figure 1

figure 2

figure 3

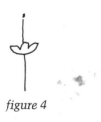

figure 4

figure 5

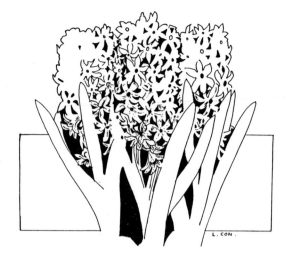

HYACINTH
HYACINTHUS ORIENTALIS

A bulbous plant native to the Mediterranean region and Asia Minor, Hyacinth derives its name from the Greek myth in which Apollo accidentally kills Hyakinthos, causing the flowers to spring from the ground whereon his blood is spilt. The numerous fragrant flowers come in white and many rich colours including every shade of blue and mauve, pink, red and yellow. They are excellent as filler flowers in arrangements.

Parts of the Flower

6 petals on trumpeted stem

Tools and Materials

hyacinth cutter
wire cutter
28-gauge wire
gum paste
gum glue
dusting colours
spatula
rolling pin and board
cornstarch
white fat
wooden stick

Method

Step 1. Make a bulb at the end of the paste and roll it out very thinly, using the "Mexican Hat" method. *See figure 1.* Cut out the flower. *See figure 2.*

Step 2. Take the wooden stick and press each petal over your finger. *See figure 3.* Again, using the wooden stick, slightly hollow out the centre of each petal. *See figure 4.*

Step 3. Make a small hook at the end of the wire. *See figure 5.* Dip the hook into the gum glue and pull through the flower. *See figure 6.* Let dry.

Step 4. To finish, group the flowers together in a cluster or use single flowers as fillers in arrangements. To dust the flowers, take the colour of the flower and dust from the centre to the outer petals.

figure 1

figure 2

figure 3

figure 4

figure 5

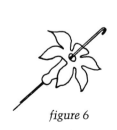

figure 6

LILY OF THE VALLEY
CONVALLARIA MAJALIS

Native to the temperate valleys of Europe and Britain, this delicate flower with its tiny white bell-shaped blossoms is ideal as a filler flower for bridal bouquets and arrangements for summer weddings. It looks especially attractive when combined with Lilacs and Roses, accented with Variegated Ivy.

Parts of the Flower

6 petals, bell-shaped

Tools and Materials

lily of the valley cutter
2 wire cutters (large and small)
28-gauge wire
gum paste
gum glue
dusting colours
small ball tool
spatula
rolling pin and board
cornstarch
white fat
very small-headed green stamens
small piece of foam

Method

Step 1. Roll out paste very thinly. Using the smallest cutter, cut out the flower. *See figure 1.* Place the flower on the foam and, with the small ball tool, stroke the petals toward the centre of the flower. (The flower should become cup-like in shape.) *See figure 2.*

Step 2. Dip the head of one of the stamens into the gum glue. *See figure 3.* Thread the stamen through the centre of the flower. *See figure 4.* Let dry.

Step 3. Repeat Steps 1 and 2 using the largest cutter. *See figure 5.*

Step 4. To assemble, tape up to 12 of the flowers together on a wire, slightly bending each flower over like a bell. *See figure 6.*

figure 1

figure 2

figure 3

figure 4

figure 5

figure 6

MINIATURE CYMBIDIUM ORCHID

Like the large Cymbidium, the miniature varieties have the characteristic boat-like lip. Originally from Asia and Australia, Miniature Cymbidiums were first cultivated in 1830. The exquisitely marked, multi-coloured blooms come in every shade except blue. As this flower is very small, it makes an excellent filler flower to compliment larger Cymbidiums or Roses accented with Ivy for greenery.

Parts of the Flower

column, throat, petals, 3 sepals

Tools and Materials

orchid cutters
wire cutters
26-gauge wire
gum paste
gum glue
dusting colours
ball tool
spatula
rolling pin and board
cornstarch
white fat
X-acto knife
apple tray
Royal icing
#1 tip
wooden anger tool

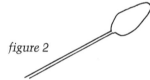

figure 1

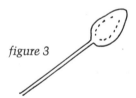

figure 2

figure 3

figure 4

figure 5

figure 6

figure 7

Method

Step 1. To Make Column:
Note: The column of an orchid should never be longer than the distance from the bottom tip of the throat cutter to the first scallop.
Take 24-gauge wire and make a hook at one end. *See figure 1.* Place a small amount of gum paste onto the hook and taper the end slightly. *See figure 2.* Flatten the column a little and curl it around the bottom end of the wooden anger tool. *See figure 3.* With the X-acto knife, mark around the tip of the column. *See figure 4.* Let dry.

Step 2. To Make Throat:
Roll out gum paste and cut out the throat. *See figure 5.* With the anger tool, ruffle the scalloped edge. *See figure 6.*

Step 3. To Attach Throat to Column:
Paint the sides and base of the column with gum glue. *See figure 7.* Attach the throat to the column at the sides and base only. *See figure 8.* Let dry.

Step 4. To Make Petals:
Roll out gum paste very thinly and cut out petals. With the X-acto knife, mark down the centre of each petal. *See figure 9.* Thin around the edges with a ball tool. *See figure 10.* Paint the centre of the petals with gum glue. *See figure 11.* Thread the wire through the centre of the petals. *See figure 12.* Shape the petals and let dry in an apple tray.

Step 5. To Assemble Flower:
With Royal icing, pipe 2 fine lines from the base of the throat into an open 'V' shape. *See figure 13.* Let dry. Paint dots on the throat with a non-toxic felt tip pen. Hi-light the throat with non-toxic chalks. See completed flower.

figure 13

figure 12

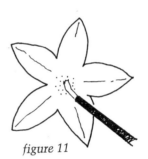

figure 11

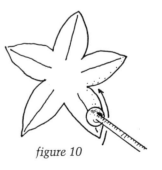

figure 10

figure 8

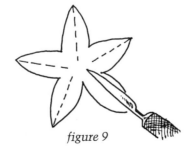

figure 9

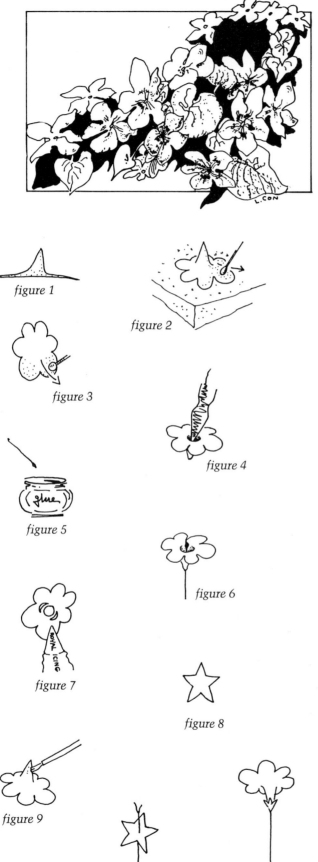

figure 1

figure 2

figure 3

figure 4

figure 5

figure 6

figure 7

figure 8

figure 9

figure 10

figure 11

VIOLET
VIOLA ODORATA

Native to Europe, Africa and Asia, the Sweet Violet or English Violet has very deep violet, or less commonly, white or rose-pink, flowers. They make excellent filler flowers for Easter cakes or for arrangements for spring or early summer garden weddings and look particularly attractive when combined with Lily of the Valley and Forget-me-nots.

Parts of the Flower

6 petals, calyx

Tools and Materials

violet cutter
calyx cutter
wire cutter
gum paste (in colour of choice)
gum glue
dusting colours
small ball tool
spatula
rolling pin and board
cornstarch
white fat
small piece of foam
small-headed yellow stamens
white Royal icing
#0 tip
wooden stick

Method

Step 1. Roll out gum paste very thinly, "Mexican Hat" style. *See figure 1.*

Step 2. Cut out violet, shape and place the flower face down on the foam. With the small ball tool, stroke the top petals away from the centre of the flowers. *See figure 2.*

Step 3. Stroke the lower petals away from the centre (to stretch and thin the leaves). *See figure 3.*

Step 4. Take the wooden stick and slightly hollow out the centre of the flower. *See figure 4.*

Step 5. Dip the head of the stamen into the gum glue. *See figure 5.*

Step 6. Thread the stamen through the centre of the flower, leaving the tip of the stamen slightly above the flower. *See figure 6.* Let dry.

Step 7. Hold the flower in one hand and, with Royal icing, pipe a half circle on either side of the protruding stamen. *See figure 7.* Let dry.

Step 8. Roll out moss green gum paste very thinly, and cut out the calyx. *See figure 8.* Paint the base of the flower with gum glue. *See figure 9.* Pull the wire through the calyx. *See figure 10.* Attach the calyx to the base of the flower. *See figure 11.* Let dry.

LEAVES

CALLA LILY LEAF

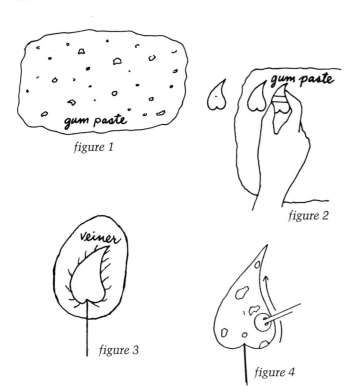

figure 1

figure 2

figure 3

figure 4

Tools and Materials

calla lily leaf cutter
wire cutter   ball tool
28-gauge wire   spatula
moss green gum paste   rolling pin and board
white gum paste   cornstarch
gum glue   white fat
green dusting colour   veiner

Method

Step 1. Roll out the green gum paste not too thinly. Place at random over the green paste small pieces of white gum paste. *See figure 1.* Continue rolling out the paste leaving a slightly thicker portion at the centre of the base through which a wire can be threaded. Cut out the leaf. *See figure 2.*

Step 2. Very gently thread the 28-gauge wire through the thicker base of the leaf to approximately ½" (1.5 cm) along the length of the leaf. Vein the petals. *See figure 3.*

Step 3. With the ball tool, roll the edges of the petal. *See figure 4.* Shape the petals as desired. Let dry. When dry, lightly dust the leaf. Steam over a boiling kettle to achieve a shiny finish.

GREEN IVY

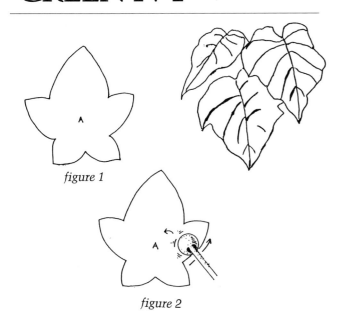

figure 1

figure 2

Tools and Materials

ivy leaf cutter
wire cutter
28-gauge wire
moss green gum paste
gum glue
dusting colours (various shades of green)
ball tool
spatula
rolling pin and board
cornstarch
white fat
veiner

Method

Step 1. Roll out the gum paste thinly leaving a small thick area at the base of the leaf through which the wire can be threaded. *See figure 1.* Thread the wire approximately ½" (1 cm) into this thicker base, taking care not to break the leaf. Vein the leaf. With a ball tool, thin around the edges. *See figure 2.*

Step 2. Dust the dry leaf with different shades of green. Hold over a steaming kettle to bring out a shine. Let dry.

ROSE LEAF

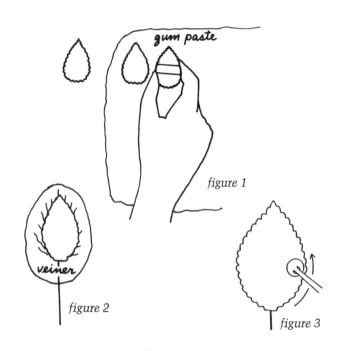

figure 1

figure 2

figure 3

VARIEGATED IVY
HEDERA HELIX AUREO-VARIEGATA

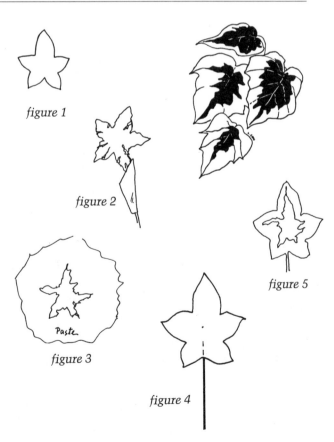

figure 1

figure 2

figure 3

figure 4

figure 5

Tools and Materials

rose leaf cutter
wire cutter
28-gauge wire
moss green gum paste
gum glue
green, red and brown
  dusting colours

ball tool
spatula
rolling pin and board
cornstarch
white fat
veiner

Method

Step 1. Roll out the moss green gum paste leaving a slightly thicker portion at the centre of the base through which a wire can be threaded. Cut out the rose leaf. *See figure 1.*

Step 2. Very gently thread the 28-gauge wire through the thicker base of the leaf to approximately ½" (1.5 cm) along the length of the leaf. Vein the leaf. *See figure 2.*

Step 3. Roll the edges of the rose leaf with the ball tool. *See figure 3.* Shape as desired and let dry.

Step 4. When dry, dust the leaf with moss green colour. Dust the edges with a little brown and red colour. Dust the underside of the leaf with red colour. Steam over a boiling kettle to obtain a shine.

Native to Europe, Asia and North Africa, Ivy is popularly used as greenery in floral arrangements for weddings and in arrangements of Orchids or Roses. This particular variety comes in white and green or creamy yellow and green.

Tools and Materials

ivy leaf cutter
wire cutter
28-gauge wire
moss green gum paste
white and yellow
  gum paste
gum glue
dusting colours

ball tool
spatula
rolling pin and board
cornstarch
white fat
styrofoam dummy
veiner

Method

Step 1. Roll out white or yellow gum paste, very thinly and cut out the leaf. *See figure 1.* Take the X-acto knife and completely misshape the outside of the leaf. *See figure 2.* Set aside. Roll out green gum paste very thinly and place the white or yellow leaf on top. *See figure 3.*

Step 2. Cut out the ivy leaf and then vein it. Thread the wire through the centre of the leaf, taking care not to break through the leaf. *See figure 4.* To shape the leaf, either dry it over a small piece of cotton wool or shape its sides with your fingers, then dry it on a styrofoam dummy. *See figure 5.* When dry, dust the ivy leaf with yellow, green or brown, then hold over a steaming kettle to give it a sheen. Do not hold it too long or it will wilt. If it isn't as shiny as you would like after one steaming, let it dry and resteam.